D1716130

ANTIQUE Santa Claus COLLECTIBLES

identification & value guide

David Longest

COLLECTOR BOOKS
A Division of Schroeder Publishing Co., Inc.

On the front cover:
Top right: Composition Santa with early papier mâché reindeer, 12" long. 400.00 – 600.00 for set.
Top row: Tall celluloid Santa Claus figure, 8". $210.00 – 275.00. Head-in-stocking decoration, 5". $125.00 – 200.00. Santa cloth and composition dolls, 5". $200.00 – 250.00.
Bottom row: Painted ceramic planter, 7" long. $65.00 – 100.00. Early composition and cloth doll with wool beard, 24". $750.00 – 1,000.00. Mercury clip ornament, 1900s. $75.00 – 95.00. Composition (chalk) statue, 10". $150.00 – 225.00.

On the back cover:
Top: Tin windup, Santa Claus on tricycle, with celluloid balloon, Japan. $125.00 – 175.00.
Top row: Blue and silver foil Santa, composition and paper. $75.00 – 95.00. Bank, spaghetti-type hat trim, 8" tall. $65.00 – $100.00.
Bottom row: German manufactured bisque and cloth doll, rare with lantern. $700.00 – 1,100.00.

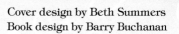

Cover design by Beth Summers
Book design by Barry Buchanan

COLLECTOR BOOKS
P.O. Box 3009
Paducah, Kentucky 42002-3009

www.collectorbooks.com

Copyright © 2009 David Longest

Searching for a Publisher?

We are always looking for people knowledgeable within their fields. If you feel that there is a real need for a book on your collectible subject and have a large comprehensive collection, contact Collector Books.

Proudly printed and bound in the United States of America

CONTENTS

ACKNOWLEDGMENTS

No book on collectibles is ever a totally solo effort. Every collector who writes about any subject owes a debt of gratitude to all the previous dealers and collectors who have contributed to his education. This book is no exception.

In particular, I would like to thank the dealers and advanced collectors who contributed their time, their expertise, and photographs of their collections for this book. When I first proposed this book back in early 2007, I suspected that my own personal collection and those collections of others' that I already knew of might make up a sample of three to four hundred Santas. As word of this book spread, and we picked up more known collectors, I am happy to say that our sample nearly doubled, to over 700 photographs.

It is my sincere hope that Santa collectors in particular and general antique dealers alike will find this book useful in identifying the many wonderful, varied items that are out there in the collecting marketplace. And remember, none of this would have been possible without the friendship, encouragement, and welcoming spirit of the contributing collectors who made this book possible.

First, I would like to thank "Butch" and Linda Miller for being the original antique Santa collectors who inspired my wife, Ann, and myself to also fall in love with antique likenesses of good old Saint Nick. Butch is a successful antique auctioneer in Southern Indiana, and his wife, Linda, taught elementary school with my wife for several decades. They are the truest of friends. I was welcomed into their home, we packed up their Santas, and I was able to get a controlled shoot of their dozens of rare old items in my own photo studio. Their trust and generosity in allowing me to cart away their treasures for several hours will always be appreciated. And, once again, I have to give credit where credit is due. It was their collection that inspired my wife and I to begin putting together our own particular antique Santa collection.

Second, I have to give a warm round of thanks to Ken and Kathy Raymond. They are fellow antiquing friends of Butch and Linda's; I hadn't talked to Ken in probably five or six years when I gave him that crazy phone call on a Sunday afternoon which amounted to, more or less, "Ken! I need your Santas!" Ken and Kathy welcomed me into their home, and we made our way through scores of Santas during a long evening, all while Kathy continued dinner preparations without a hitch. It was a fun night! Many of the very fine early composition Santas pictured in the book are from Ken and Kathy's collection.

Next, I thank the most enthusiastic contributor to this book, California collector Diane Savage. Diane had been a little under the weather when I approached her with the idea of this book. Actually, we met through the purchase of a wonderful and large antique Santa that appears on the cover of this book, front and center. He's the one with the rippled wool beard and bright felt clothes who is looking to the left. That old Santa brought Diane and me together. She got Santa shipped to my house in plenty of time to be a Christmas present for my wife, and through becoming my sort of eBay pen-pal, she disclosed that she had been collecting hundreds of Santas over the years, from many different eras. The only problem was, they were all boxed and put away. Being the true collector extraordinaire that she is (in addition to being one heck of a nice person!), Diane agreed to pull out her hundreds of Santas from storage and add their photographs to this book. Her voluntary efforts gave this book an expanse that it would not otherwise have had. I will always be indebted to her for her kind encouragement, support, and help that went far beyond the line of duty. You can find Diane's email contact information (in addition to the contacts for many of the the other contributing collectors to this book) in the collector's resource chapter at the end of this book.

Jim and Bonnie Kasari are two other dear friends who also allowed me to shoot their Santa collections. Now, Jim and Bonnie are a book unto themselves. Nearly every holiday from New Year's through Christmas finds the Kasari home decorated lavishly for the spirit of whatever is being observed. Easter, Halloween, the Fourth of July, you name it, the Kasaris decorate their house from wall to wall. Jim puts together an elaborate Coca-Cola Christmas village with running trains, vehicles, fountains, waterfalls, and a citizenry of hundreds that takes weeks to assemble. Their upstairs boasts themed Christmas trees in absolutely every room, including outhouse Christmas decorations in their bathrooms! If there ever were Spirits of Christmas Present, they would be Jim and Bonnie Kasari. Many of the Coca-Cola Santa collectibles and nutcrackers are from their collection. Thanks to both of you, Bonnie and Jim. You are the living embodiment of Christmas spirit.

Mr. and Mrs. Norman Stockton of Indiana were most gracious hosts in midwinter, when they retrieved their mother's amazing collection from storage and allowed me to photograph it. Also, some of the very fine Victorian dolls and pieces are from the collection of Jeanne Weaver, whom I never met, but who graciously allowed me to photograph her treasures. So, to the Stocktons and to Jean, I hope you will enjoy seeing your fine old family heirlooms as they appear in the book, and please know that your help and the trouble you went to will always be tremendously appreciated.

Elmer and Viola Reynolds, of Indiana, have been involved in some way in all nine of my books on collecting toys. From the first day I met them at a country auction, we were like family. And by the time this book is released, we will have spent 27 years together seeking that which is old, and fun, and seemingly always new. It is their vintage Coca-Cola display advertising featuring Santa that appears in the book, and some very substantial dolls and decorations appear as well. What can I say, Elmer and Viola, you have been and always remain there for me. Your help with this book is, as always, much appreciated, but your friendship is forever treasured.

Also, many thanks go out to Charlie Douglas and Tom Luce, of New Albany, Indiana, for allowing me access to their collection right at Christmastime. They, too, are dear friends.

The friendly folks of Santa Claus, Indiana, have to warrant the Charming Town of the Year award for their help in steering me in the right direction with my requests for this book. The Santa Claus Museum at Kringle Plaza allowed my intrusion for a day; I had Santas and toys spread out on the floor, along with all of my photography mess. I hope the book will make you proud! Special thanks to the Santa Claus Museum director, Crystal Buehler, who was most welcoming; to Paula Werne, director of public relations for Holiday World, who pointed me in all the right directions; and last but never least, Pat Koch, referred to affectionately over the years as "Santa's daughter," who helped put Santa Claus on the map and established the Santa Claus Museum in the first place.

The whole gang at Collector Books gets a tip of my hat for giving me a couple of deadline extensions just when I needed them and for creating, once again, a beautiful book. Special thanks to the world's most understanding (and kind!) editor, Gail Ashburn, along with Amy Sullivan and the rest of the very fine folks who always roll up their sleeves on the day the manuscript arrives and somehow make a fine book out of it all. Have you ever wondered what 715 photographs spread around a table look like? Believe me, Gail and Amy know! Thanks also to Billy Schroeder, publisher at Collector Books, for over a quarter of a century of faith in me and for publishing this book number nine.

As always, I thank my wife, Ann, and daughter, Claire, for sharing in the love of Santa Claus for many years and for being encouraging and even prodding when I needed a little push. This guy would not be who he is without his two wonderful girls. I love you both!

The eight books that came before this one were all special to me in their own way, but this one is very dear to my heart. I knew Santa Claus before I ever knew Mickey Mouse or Huckleberry Hound, and to work on a book on the subject of this wonderful old gentleman and the merchandise his legacy inspired, well, let's say it has been a tremendous honor. When I was six years old, something awakened me in the very early hours of Christmas morning. My bedroom was in the back of our house, and I had to climb a small stairway to peer up into our living room. I never turned on a light, but the moonlight shining through our picture window illuminated the Christmas tree and the man standing in front of it. It wasn't anyone in my family — I would have turned on the light and spoken to him. In perfect silhouette against the moonlight, it was a man with a beard and a round belly, and I could hear the slight ding of the bells on his boots. I swear this happened. I still see him as plainly as if daylight were illuminating the scene.

I never asked my parents who that was in the middle of the night. I didn't want to spoil it. As brief as it was, that was my own special one-on-one with St. Nick. And it will always remain with me.

Finally, I thank the spirit of human generosity and kindness that is Santa Claus. In essence, this is his book, not mine. We all love you, Santa. May every day be Christmas.

INTRODUCTION

Santa Claus has arrived on the collecting scene. When it comes to Americana, he's as American as apple pie and the proverbial girl next door. But he is much more than a collectible figurine, an antique curiosity, or holiday icon. Santa Claus is a symbol of spirit. Consider the fact that nearly every American household (including many who don't even celebrate the religious holiday of Christmas) has Santa collectibles stored away with holiday decorations in some out-of-reach box in an attic or basement. Many families have passed Santa decorations and collectibles down from one generation to the next, starting a multifamily, multigenerational collection that may last for centuries. Santa's likeness is the most recognized fictional character in all of Western civilization traditions, so is it any wonder that literally millions of Santa items are stored, preserved, treasured, passed on, and collected every year?

In the truest spirit of that frigid North Pole where Santa lives, this book will only present a tip-of-the-iceberg approach to Santa antiques and collectibles. Since the 1890s through the present, literally tens of thousands of Santa Claus items have been marketed. This book will give both the novice and the advanced collector a perspective on what types of Santa items are actually available to resourceful buyers, while also offering an informal timeline and when and where Santa items were manufactured. Finally, the book will offer a price range in today's market values for every item pictured.

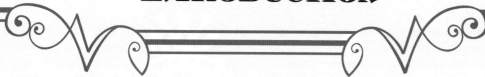

One of the easiest ways to identify the time periods of manufacture for Santa items is by construction material. Most very antique-looking paper lithographed items were manufactured just prior to the turn of the century up until about 1910. Celluloid (or, as it is often referred to, cellulose) items began to be manufactured in the 1920s, but became the most popular Santa medium during the late 1930s and on through the 1940s. Hard and shiny plastics appeared in the late 1940s and were used for Santa items well into the 1960s. Composition and plaster-faced cloth-bodied Santas were manufactured in Japan in the 1930s and 1940s up until World War II, and these are often mistaken as being Victorian Santa collectibles from around the turn of the century. They are not. Although these dime-store-type Santa figures have the look of being over 100 years old because of the primitive appearance of the Santa faces, along with the detailed cloth wardrobes they wear, in truth they are collectible figures from some three and four decades later. Bisque (or kiln-fired white clay) figures were manufactured in both Japan and Germany from just after the dawn of the 1900s up until the 1950s. After that time period, most Santa figures became highly glazed and brightly painted commercial ceramic pieces.

A one-paragraph summary of Santa Claus manufacturing materials is a rather cursory education as to the age of items pictured in this book, but it should help the reader as a general guide to determining the origin of items as they are found in the collecting marketplace.

One way not to determine the true age of a Santa is by its general style or appearance. In recent years, because of the increasing demand for vintage "Victorian" and turn-of-the-century Santas, the worldwide market has produced scores of expertly rendered reproductions. Many of these reproductions even have archaic dates such as "1880" or "1910" molded into the bases of the figurines. Rarely, I repeat, rarely were dates ever place on very early Santas of 100 years ago. It just wasn't done, since there was no apparent lasting historical value for doing this. Santa collectibles hadn't been around long enough for anyone to think it noteworthy enough to hallmark Santa figurines and collectibles in the late 1800s or early 1900s with any date. An exact date molded into any such item usually indicates that it is likely a recent reproduction done in an antiqued or vintage style.

Santa Claus collecting is extremely popular today because Christmas and holiday collectibles are a popular genre of collecting in general. Santa Claus collectibles appeal to general antique collectors, holiday antique collectors, Christmas decoration collectors, Americana and folklore collectors, and even children's item and toy collectors. Santa collecting is a lasting, significant, and specific branch of holiday memorabilia collecting. What makes Santa collectibles popular is also the availability of the items. Any household of the past 100 years that put up a Christmas tree probably also had a few Santa figures and toys around. And these got packed away once a year when the holidays were over, only to reappear in another eleven months or so. It is this simple fact that has allowed Santa collectibles to flourish, remain ever present, and be available to collectors in often amazing condition. The examples simply weren't out in the open for wear and tear from use for very long. Their shelf life was usually less than one month per year, so Santa toys, games, cards, figures, dolls, and ceramic pieces were exposed to the elements of young hands for only a comparatively brief time. When the holidays were over, they were also packed away carefully with loving hands. These vintage Santa items, therefore, have most fortunately lasted.

The price listing present in the caption of every item pictured in this book gives a general range. The first price listed is for the item in good but used condition, in the condition that this collectible may usually be found — its normal condition. The second price listed is for the item as it might be found in flawless, like new, factory mint condition. Very few Santa items can boast a condition that is truly mint because they were used, packed away, and then repacked year after year, Christmas after Christmas. Although they were protected each year, even careful packing over and over takes its toll. Collectors should therefore assume that most items priced in this book will realistically be in the lower price range given. The second price should only be used if an item is like new in its original box (such as found in old store stock or warehouse finds) or if it was discovered after being packed away for decades with little or no recent use at all.

The reader should assume that the prices listed are antique show prices, or the general value an item would have if sold at a legitimate general antique show. This author has not used eBay prices as a guide, because on any given night of the week, or any given month of the year, online auction prices for all Christmas collectibles in general fluctuate wildly. A word to the wise — don't buy your antique or collectible Santa items during October through early December. It's just common sense, but that is when the flourishing activity peaks as collectors, designers, decorators, store display artists, and general gift givers do their Christmas item buying. Buy and collect Santa Claus collectibles in the off season — any time from January through September. Only the most devoted collectors buy then (or even think about Santa at all), and so prices are more reasonable.

In summary, learn to identify the age of Santa items by using this book as a reference (and the many other great general guides to holiday collectibles — Collector Books offers several others) as you do your seeking, finding, and buying. Be patient, demand excellent condition of items going permanently into your collection (more will be discussed about this in the final chapter, Santa Collector's Resource Guide), and buy in the off season. Take care to keep your collection protected from wear and tear and the elements, and you should have a valuable lasting historical legacy to pass along to your heirs.

Most of us have very fond memories of Santa Claus and his importance in our childhoods. Collecting Santa Claus items is a tangible, fun, and effective way to rekindle the flame of those youthful, magical memories and moments.

Being a drama teacher by profession, I teach my students to regard every role played as an important one. Santa is near and dear to my heart, because he was the first character that I ever performed. Consider Christmas 1958. I was four years old, and my family was hosting the annual Longest Christmas Eve party. My sisters decided that it would be cute if they dressed me as Santa and let me pass out all the presents to my uncles, aunts, and a dozen cousins. My suit was red flannel pajamas stuffed with pillows, and I believe my beard was a fuzzy towel. Anyway, they gave me my lines of "HO, HO, HO," which I performed in the deepest voice a four-year-old could muster, and I must have been a hit. The flashbulbs went off in a frenzy! I remember that my bag of presents was a pillowcase, and it was truly my first experience of actual gift giving. In all, it felt very good.

Fast forward to Christmastime 1976. I was a poor college student barely able to make apartment rent and tuition, and an offer from the local chamber of commerce came to me. They wanted a young actor type to play Santa, and the pay was $500 for working the month of December — a sizable sum for a college kid. I accepted the job for two years of Decembers. The first year was the most eventful, as I sat in a small shopping boutique inside a tiny house. I visited with a lot of children, and heard a load of interesting wishes. What I learned as a young man playing Santa was that his magic knows no economic boundaries. Rich and poor children alike had the same wishes, generally. They usually dreamed about the same types of toys. What differed were the looks that I could read on the faces of the parents. Some parents nodded encouragingly, allowing a list to go on and on that was a little indulgent even for a loving Santa. Other lists were quite short, and from the looks in the eyes of the doting parents, the list might be difficult for "Santa's helpers" to make materialize. That is what bothered me the most. Here I was, all rosy cheeked and playing an almost divine character who was supposed to listen to and grant toy wishes, but knowing full well that all wishes could not be granted. So I walked a fine line. I played an encouraging old benevolent giver who would do his best to see to all wishes, yet I was guarded. I made sure that I made no promises. My answers were usually of the "Santa will do his best" or "the Elves have been working overtime and they will do all they can do" variety. And that was usually good enough, when accompanied by the small candy cane that Santa gave to everyone.

Honestly, the one thing that playing Santa for two years taught me was that I really love children. I knew as each little endearing child sat upon my lap that I was going to be a good father someday. I was 22 years old, and I quickly learned that children truly are God's greatest treasures on earth. And Christmas really does bring out the best in both children and adults. Santa Claus is one of the human spirit's greatest ambassadors. He is love and humanity at their best.

The next year, the Santa house was moved to the outdoors, and there I sat for hours and hours in December of 1977, talking with local children, my abode heated only by a tiny space heater. I sat there when I watched the bank thermometer across the street blink out five degrees below zero with blowing snow, and still the children came. In actuality, they thought I loved such weather — it was closer in line with that of the North Pole.

I mention all of this personal background only to illustrate the undying reverence I have for the spirit of St. Nick. It was truly one of the greatest joys of my life to listen for two years to the heartfelt wishes of small children. I never got my beard pulled, no child ever got sick in my presence…in truth, they were angels. My time as Santa is one of the best memories of my college years. It was a privilege to act for two months of my life as Santa's helper. And I took the role quite seriously, seriously enough that when I visited the nursing-home bedside of my 93-year-old grandmother that year, I carried on a ten-minute conversation with her before she figured out it was me! A year later, my college sweetheart and I were married, and from the beginning of our marriage, we collected Santa Claus antiques.

Certainly Santa's history runs deeper than my own. There have been countless essays and magazine articles focusing upon his origins. Most accounts point to the Christian basis for Santa Claus as being a very giving, loving, rich, and generous Bishop Nicholas of Myra in Lycia (now a part of Turkey) who lived in the fourth century AD. In these accounts, St. Nicholas is known for throwing gifts through windows to poor children, or providing poor young women with dowries so that they could marry. The death of this most loving and kind man occurred on December 6, and so it is this date that often marked the beginning of winter festivities and banquets in his honor during medieval times. As Christian influences continued in Europe during the Renaissance, this December 6 festival date came to be merged into the entire season of the Nativity, serving to make Christmas celebrations move toward the length of a multiweek season of caring and giving to begin with St. Nicholas Day and culminate with Christmas.

Our modern notion of Santa Claus finds its origins with several unique writers and artists. The earliest mention of one "St. A. Claus" is said to have appeared in colonial American newspapers as early as 1773, but Santa's real introduction to the United States came in a well-known Washington Irving work, *Diedrich Knickerbocker's History of New York*, which was published in 1809. In this work, Irving introduced the Dutch version of Saint Nicholas, who was loving and giving and rode on horseback.

In the 1823 poem "A Visit from St. Nicholas" (more commonly known as "The Night before Christmas"), Clement C. Moore introduced us to the Americanized form of Santa Claus that we know today. In his poem, Santa is described as a "jolly old elf" and flies through the sky with eight reindeer, which he names. He enters and exits houses by way of chimneys and has all the characteristics of a spirited, loving ambassador of goodwill;

he laughs out loud and winks and nods. Moore introduced Santa to the populace as a true character.

Later, from the 1860s through the 1880s, magazine and book illustrator Thomas Nast added the trappings that Santa had a workshop at the North Pole, kept a good and bad boy and girl list for the entire population of the world, and had a rather feisty disposition. Many of his illustrations can be found in issues of *Harper's Magazine* from the 1860s and the 1870s.

Finally, in the twentieth century, it was commercial artist Haddon Sundblom who did wonders for warming up Santa's image, in the Coca-Cola Santa ads, which depicted Santa as quite rotund, sharply dressed, and handsomely rosy cheeked. The first Sundblom Santa ad appeared as a large billboard in 1931.

Certainly Hollywood has added its own charm to Santa for the past century. He has been involved in intrigue, adventures, and missions of goodwill, and has been the source of small miracles. Countless other adaptations will certainly emerge as we work our way into this newer century.

Through it all, Santa will continue to warm the hearts of all who believe in Christmas, both the young and the old. He is a symbol of hope, childhood, and happiness. The spirit of Christmas lives in Santa, and through the collecting of his likeness, we are made better.

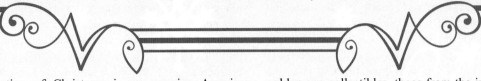

The celebration of Christmas is an amazing American tradition. Like America itself, our celebration of the holiday is a blending, a compilation, a merging of a myriad of different customs, beliefs, traditions, and practices mixed together by means of centuries of people immigrating to the United States. As a result, Christmas and Santa items today represent the very best of what everyone brought with them from the homeland, both physically and traditionally.

Scandinavian immigrants (from Denmark, Norway, and Sweden) brought the tradition of representing Saint Nicholas as a bishop, usually attired in more religious-looking garb and carrying a staff and wearing a jeweled hat, but sometimes wearing the more ornate attire of a saint. German and Central European immigrants brought with them the Belsnickle traditions, which can present Santa in any one of a dozen or more fantastic colors, with red not always being the norm as it is today. Certainly sometimes Victorian Belsknickles can be found in red, but more often than not these early figural items are adorned in tones of purple, green, yellow, gold, white, and even pink! The color of these early composition, papier maché, or chalk figurals may present great variety, but the structure of these German-inspired figures is amazingly similar in nearly all examples. Santa is presented in a rather cylindrical shape, with a straight, tall, conical hat, triangular long and thin beard, and very basic nondetailed serious-looking facial features.

A Belsnickle may or may not be holding a twig or evergreen branch symbolic of his earthy origins, but he often has a very stern countenance. Some even look outright angry. It is interesting to wonder how Victorian children might have perceived the early Belsnickle representation of Santa. Certainly not present is any warmth of the charming Santa who welcomes children into his arms. These older and very early Santa figures present Santa as meaning very serious business, possibly inspired by his rather stark history of either rewarding the very good children with sweets or treasures or leaving coal, sticks, switches, or sticks to the bad children of the world — or sometimes even passing them by and forgetting them altogether!

One of the reasons this author believes Santa collectors treasure the very serious Victorian-era Santas is because they represent the very beginning of the tradition and folklore surrounding the character. These are the baseline, the golden age collectibles, those from the inception, the start. That is why they are so treasured.

Another popular area of Santa collecting from this time period is vintage Victorian postcards with Santa Claus themes. This chapter presents many versions of these, with various depictions of Santa. Collectors sometimes wonder why there are so many styles of Victorian postcards available, and why Santa is the subject of so many. The answer is simple. Before there were Hallmark stores, there were postcards. Postcards were popular greetings for all holidays throughout the year and were sold at the turn of the century in dime stores and general stores alike. Postcards were the greeting cards of the late 1800s and early 1900s. Consequently, with Christmas being the most popular holiday of all, it comes as no surprise that collectors have a virtual treasure trove of very early postcards from this area, with wonderfully colorful and varied versions of Santa Claus on nearly all of them with Christmas themes. Embossed (or pressure stamped) cards are the most valuable, as are those with gilding or gold accents or three-dimensional textures. Cards with Santa Claus presented as traveling by airship (blimp) or other nonstandard means are very collectible, as are cards with Santa in old-time cars, with telegraph operators, or with any other character or antique item of historical significance. Many collectors also prefer depictions of Santa with small children.

A few cast-iron Santas from the turn of the century still survive today, as do a relatively small number of Victorian-era Santa Claus dolls. But collectors should note that the bulk of what many people believe are truly Victorian Santa items miss the decade at the turn of the century by some 20 to 30 years. As the next chapter will point out, most of what we have come to treasure as "antique" Santa items are actually dime-store-derived collectibles from the 1920s through the 1940s. Although Santa figures may have the look of being 100 or more years old, they often are not. The heyday of mass Santa manufacture and collecting really took hold in the Roaring Twenties and has not let up in 80 years!

When buying Victorian-era Santa items, be sure you know the dealer or the source, and be certain the item is from the period it is purported to be from. Reproductions abound in today's market because the very earliest Santas are the most desirable ones, and it is relatively easy to reproduce composition and felt items with resin figures dressed in stiff paper. The bottom line is, know the period you want to collect and become an expert as to the materials of manufacture and countries of origin. Consult fellow collectors. With an appreciation for what is truly old, the avid collector will soon be able to traverse the marketplace armed with enough knowledge to avoid the pitfalls of tempting reproductions.

Victorian Santas are the holy grail of Christmas collecting. Find one in excellent condition at a reasonable price and it is a must buy. As the cliché goes, they just don't make them like they used to.

Composition Victorian Belsnickle figure, 10". $500.00 – 750.00.

Antique composition Victorian Belsnickle Santa, 12" with sprig. $750.00 – 1,000.00.

Antique composition 10" Victorian Belsnickle figure. $800.00 – 1,000.00.

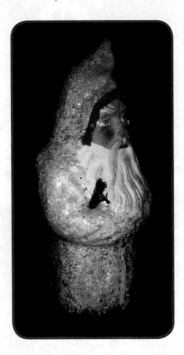

Antique composition 8" Belsnickle figure, with evergreen. $700.00 – 900.00.

Antique Belsnickle figure with sprig. $650.00 – 800.00.

Antique composition Santa, 6" with base. $200.00 – 300.00.

Antique Victorian cotton lithographed scrap ornament. $75.00 – 100.00.

Mercury clip ornament, 1900s. $75.00 – 95.00.

Antique mercury ornament, hanger style.
$50.00 – 75.00.

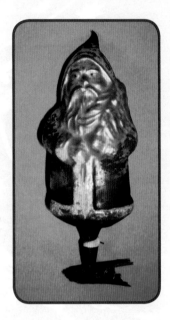

Mercury clip ornament, 1900s.
$75.00 – 95.00.

Victorian Santa, paper and cloth decoration,
1900s lithographed. $200.00 – 300.00.

Victorian and mercury tinsel lithograph scrap ornament. $50.00 – 75.00.

Mercury ornament, 1900s. $50.00 – 75.00.

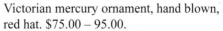

Victorian mercury ornament, hand blown, red hat. $75.00 – 95.00.

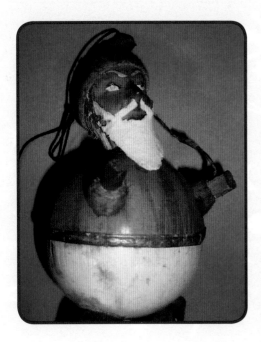

Composition Santa dangle ornament, very early.
$100.00 – 150.00.

Hand-blown Victorian ornament, 1900s.
$75.00 – 100.00.

Rare tall composition doll with leather boots and
Santa pin, 24". $1,000.00 – 1,500.00.

Antique cloth and composition doll, early, with tinsel twig, 12". $350.00 – 500.00.

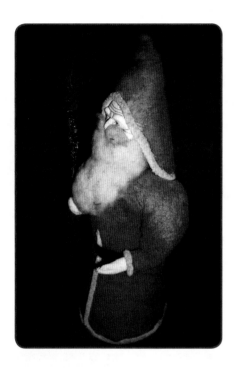

Cloth and composition doll, early. $200.00 – 300.00.

Cloth and composition doll, 5". $200.00 – 250.00.

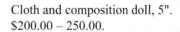

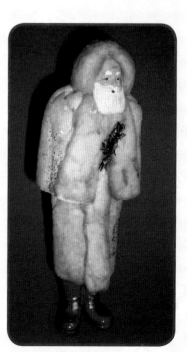

Cloth and composition doll, early, 8".
$250.00 – 350.00.

German manufactured bisque and cloth doll,
rare with lantern. $700.00 – 1,100.00.

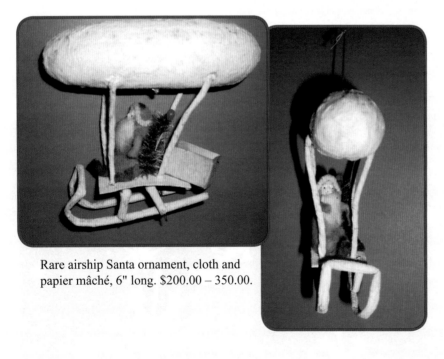

Rare airship Santa ornament, cloth and
papier mâché, 6" long. $200.00 – 350.00.

Cloth and composition figure, early, 6".
$175.00 – 275.00.

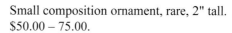

Small composition ornament, rare, 2" tall. $50.00 – 75.00.

Cloth and composition doll (ornament, no base), early, 5". $150.00 – 250.00.

Cloth and composition ornament. $125.00 – 175.00.

Early composition and cloth doll with wool beard, 24". $750.00 – 1,000.00.

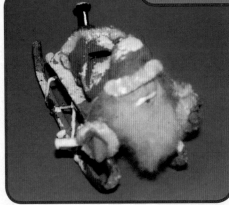

Santa Claus on sled figure, 6" long, rare. $200.00 – 300.00.

Lithographed scrap ornament with mercury tinsel.
$50.00 – 75.00.

Cast-iron sleigh with reindeer and composition/cloth
Santa. $800.00 – 1,000.00.

Composition Santa on wooden sled with
presents and bag. $400.00 – 600.00.

Composition and cloth figure, early, 6" tall.
$150.00 – 250.00.

Composition stick decoration, early, 3"
long. $75.00 – 100.00.

Rare old composition Santa, 6", wool felt
clothes, early. $150.00 – 225.00.

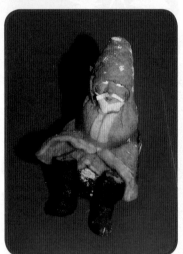

Old composition candy container, Santa seated on
stump, rare. $300.00 – 450.00.

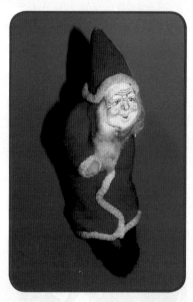

Unusual clownlike vintage figure, early, 6"
tall. $150.00 – 275.00.

Early 1900s vintage China plate, Santa
with children, 8". $75.00 – 100.00.

Composition Santa with papier mâché early reindeer, set, 12" long. $400.00 – 600.00.

Very large cloth and wool felt doll with cloth face, rare, 30". $1,000.00 – 1,250.00.

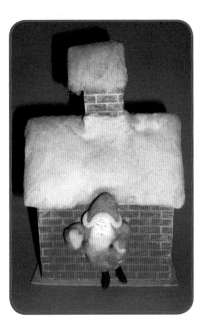

Cloth and composition early Santa in Victorian-style house, rare. $250.00 – 350.00.

Early composition Santa in chimney, pop-up-type toy, 7" tall. $350.00 – 450.00.

Composition Santa with early papier mâché reindeer, set, 12" long. $400.00 – 600.00.

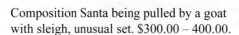

Composition Santa being pulled by a goat with sleigh, unusual set. $300.00 – 400.00.

Composition Santa being pulled by a horse, rare figures, unusual pair. $350.00 – 450.00.

Old composition Santa figure with evergreen branch, 5" tall, early. $175.00 – 275.00.

Primitive-looking early composition/chalk Santa on base and with bag, 6". $250.00 – 350.00.

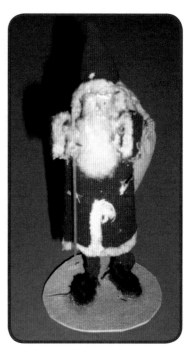

Old composition Santa, 5", with long staff or cane and wool beard. $225.00 – 275.00.

Small composition and cloth Santa with star for belt buckle. $125.00 – 175.00.

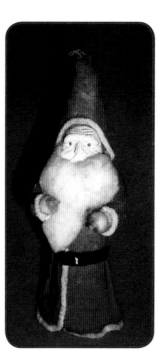

Early cloth and composition Santa, 6", with bushy cotton beard. $150.00 – 250.00.

North Pole Wireless Christmas postcard, 1900s. $35.00 – 55.00.

"A Christmas Greeting" postcard from 1912 with Santa in airship, rare. $75.00 – 100.00.

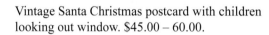

Vintage Santa Christmas postcard with children looking out window. $45.00 – 60.00.

"Christmas Greetings" postcard, Santa in rare purple suit, 1900s, gold. $40.00 – 60.00.

Santa Claus postcard, 1900s. $25.00 – 50.00.

"A Bright and Cheery Christmas" postcard, 1900s. $25.00 – 50.00.

Very early Santa and child Christmas postcard. $25.00 – 50.00.

Very early Santa and child Christmas postcard. $25.00 – 50.00.

"A Merry Christmas" postcard with unusual black or dark-skinned Santa. $75.00 – 100.00.

Victorian Santa Christmas card with rabbit.
$25.00 – 50.00.

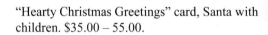

"Hearty Christmas Greetings" card, Santa with
children. $35.00 – 55.00.

Unusual embossed or stamped ornate Santa
Christmas card. $75.00 – 100.00.

Santa Claus in chimney Christmas postcard.
$35.00 – 55.00.

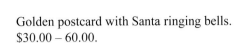

Golden postcard with Santa ringing bells. $30.00 – 60.00.

"A Joyous Christmas" postcard with Santa reading letter, early. $35.00 – 55.00.

Santa Claus with holly Victorian Christmas postcard. $35.00 – 55.00.

Embossed Christmas postcard, Santa with candy canes. $40.00 – 65.00.

Santa "Dreams" card, unusual art, Santa in hearth fire, sleeping child, rare. $45.00 – 75.00.

Santa visiting children and begging dog Christmas postcard. $35.00 – 55.00.

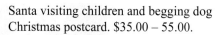

Christmas postcard, Santa with toy. $25.00 – 50.00.

Santa with Christmas punch postcard. $25.00 – 50.00.

Postcard, Santa with toys and visiting sleeping child. $35.00 – 60.00.

Christmas postcard, Santa holding globe and with toys and bells. $30.00 – 60.00.

"A Christmas Reverie" gold lithographed early postcard. $35.00 – 65.00.

Little girl with Santa "Happy New Year" postcard. $30.00 – 60.00.

Santa visiting child and maid by airship, toys floating, unusual! $75.00 – 100.00.

Santa flocked postcard with bookmark ribbon, unusual. $30.00 – 60.00.

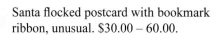

Postcard, Santa and girl with Christmas tree. $30.00 – 60.00.

Old-time Santa, Victorian card with bells, gold. $35.00 – 65.00.

Early Santa postcard. $25.00 – 50.00.

Santa dressed in unusual silver robe with old toys, very old, rare. $55.00 – 85.00.

Santa with children, die-cut place card or greeting card. $30.00 – 55.00.

Santa Claus at chimney, "A Merry Christmas" postcard. $25.00 – 50.00.

The Night before Christmas book, rare, 1900s. $75.00 – 125.00.

Christmas Delights Victorian cloth (possibly linen) book, 1890s. $100.00 – 150.00.

The Night before Christmas, large storybook, c. 1908 by Wood Publishers. $110.00 – 165.00.

The Night before Christmas, large storybook, c. 1908 by Wood Publishers. $110.00 – 165.00.

The Night before Christmas, large storybook, c. 1908 by Wood Publishers. $110.00 – 165.00.

The Night before Christmas, large storybook, c. 1908 by Wood Publishers. $110.00 – 165.00.

The Night before Christmas, large storybook, c. 1908 by Wood Publishers. $110.00 – 165.00.

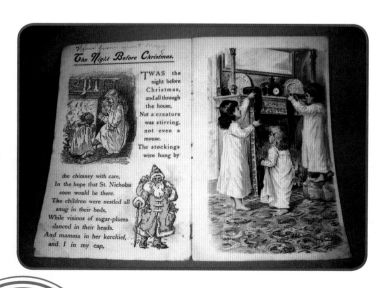

The Night before Christmas, large storybook, c. 1908 by Wood Publishers. $110.00 – 165.00.

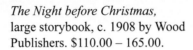

The Night before Christmas, large storybook, c. 1908 by Wood Publishers. $110.00 – 165.00.

Figural Victorian Santa ornament, early. $75.00 – 100.00.

Scrap lithograph Victorian ornament with glass ball and tinsel. $45.00 – 65.00.

Early blown glass ornament, gold face, rare. $85.00 – 110.00.

Figural ornament, early. $65.00 – 90.00.

Composition and cloth doll with rope and bag. $110.00 – 180.00.

Santa Claus with globe postcard. $30.00 – 60.00.

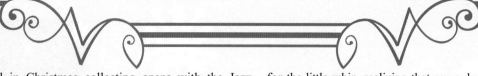

This period in Christmas collecting opens with the Jazz Age of the Roaring Twenties, when cars were getting bigger and bigger, ladies' hemlines were on the way up, F. Scott Fitzgerald was the hottest literary personage around, and dime stores began springing up on even the tiniest of Main Streets in the smallest of towns. As affluence was on the rise, families had more expendable income and the big crash on Wall Street was almost a decade away. We had just won World War I, and America was out to have some fun. And one of the ways to celebrate was to make Christmas more special than it had ever been before. In the 1920s, our celebration of the holiday began to take on a broader meaning than that of only a religious celebration — it was to become a true season of revelry. This meant that we would now buy more, decorate more, celebrate more, and collect more — thus ensuring that our traditions with Santa and his collectibles were here to stay!

The dime-store collectibles of the 1920s and 1930s presented to the average American family decorative holiday items that were both inexpensive and appealing to the eye. Certainly at the top of the list of items available were Santa figurines made of celluloid. This substance was an early precursor to modern plastics and had a short lifespan mainly because of its extremely lightweight and fragile properties. Truly, some of these items were daintier than if they had been constructed from an eggshell. Celluloid items are extremely susceptible to heat damage (they are made from a derivative of organic camphor) and melt down easily in attic heat or direct sunlight. They are also highly flammable. They can also crunch into unrecognizable pieces if stepped upon or smashed. Consequently, many of these great figural items didn't last for the many decades it would take to sustain them to the present day. Those that have survived are valuable and extremely collectible, particularly those without any blemishes or damage.

The onset of the late 1940s and 1950s would see developments in true man-made plastics that would prove much more durable than celluloid, and these examples would last much longer. Collectors of 1920s and 1930s celluloid Santa figures should take great care in the packing away of these items. This past season, I purchased an exquisite large Santa Claus in a celluloid sleigh being pulled by two large white reindeer. The condition of this entire example was exceptional. However, when packing it away for the season (the first time I had personally owned it and packed it away!) I noticed that Santa's tiny whip (which was also celluloid) was missing from the palm of his hand. I searched high and low for this tiny piece, knowing that if I didn't find it, the vacuum cleaner would probably do away with it forever. Celluloid is just so extremely lightweight, it is almost like the toy doesn't exist in matter at all. It's like the lemon meringue of plastic! I searched and searched for the little whip, realizing that my only hope would probably be to fabricate some sort of a replacement for this missing piece next Christmas. I gave the Santa figure one last rattle before packing it away, and I noticed an unusual sound. You guessed it! The whip had withdrawn back through the hole in the palm of Santa's hand and was now seemingly forever trapped inside his body. With the patience one would use to solve a difficult puzzle, I shook the figure at different angles for about 15 minutes and the whip emerged. I immediately reglued it so this event didn't transpire again next year, and now whip and Santa figure are merged together as one. I mention this only to illustrate the fragility of celluloid items. Making a decision to collect these wonderfully colorful and bright items is also a decision to destine yourself to after-holiday packing that requires special care and patience. But the celluloid figural Santas are just so wonderful, they are worth it.

Particular care should also be taken when collecting the many composition-faced Santa dolls from dime stores of this period. Most of the tiny Santa dolls pictured in this chapter feature cloth or paper clothing on a wire or pipe-cleaner Santa body frame and have a composition or celluloid head. These "antique" Santa figures are often mistaken for being much, much older than they actually are. Many collectors purchase these because of their old German look, thinking that they are extremely old handmade items. In truth, most of these were made in Japan starting in the 1920s and were manufactured through the 1940s, and although they look very old, they are certainly not collectibles from the late 1800s!

Many of the large figural Santa items pictured in this book are also from this time period. Large chalk Santa statues were usually given as carnival prizes, and the more detailed composition (wood mixed with glue!) examples are usually from the 1930s or early 1940s. These, too, are often mistaken for being from the Victorian era. They are not.

Several very large dolls with composition or cloth faces are pictured in this chapter, and these date from the 1920s, but also have a much earlier look. When collecting items of such a substantial size and those that are principally cloth in structure, collectors should take very special care in packing these items away for the long months between holidays. Areas where we store our holiday items can often be quite damp, dark, and remote, and this encourages damage from both insects and rodents. Plastic tubs sealed off with cellophane tape and stored high and dry in climate- and humidity-controlled storage areas are the ideal. When these aren't available, at least avoid attics and basements. Valuable Christmas collectibles, and fragile Santas in particular, do much better inside the house in storage closets, where both temperature and humidity are more stable.

Santa collectibles from the 1920s and the 1930s are still some of the best antique bargains available to collectors today. Because the dime-store designs were so plentifully distributed (let's face it, these were sold to the stores by the gross — that's 144 at a time!), they are still readily available and rather easy to find in the marketplace. This simple fact of supply and demand keeps prices reasonable, so often it is possible to buy Santa items from this time period for about the same prices they had in the 1950s or 1960s. Quite honestly, the people who were the original purchasers of these items (adults who were buying in the 1920s or the 1930s) were born in the 1900s, so many of them are gone now. Even children from the 1920s through

the 1930s are getting up in their years now, and probably not buying back their memories at this stage in their lives. This factor creates a gap. And where there is a gap, there are bargains to be found. More buying adults at the present have a stronger attachment to Santas from the 1940s through the 1960s, so this drives prices *up*. Fewer people have actual associations with Santa collectibles from the 1920s and 1930s at present, so this helps to stabilize prices. Bear this in mind when you negotiate in the marketplace. When it comes to Santa items from these two decades, it is always a buyer's market!

Ornate windup music box on base, composition and cloth. $200.00 – 350.00.

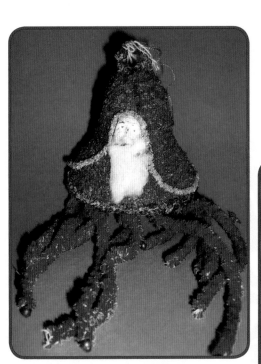

Early chenille bell with composition Santa face. $150.00 – 275.00.

Head-in-stocking decoration, 5".
$125.00 – 200.00.

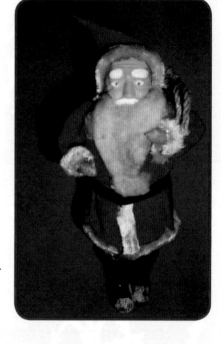

Composition and cloth figure, 5".
$125.00 – 200.00.

Unusual silver foil paper and composition
Santa. $150.00 – 250.00.

Celluloid, cloth, and composition Santa, 4".
$125.00 – 150.00.

Cloth and composition doll or ornament, cotton
beard. $125.00 – 175.00.

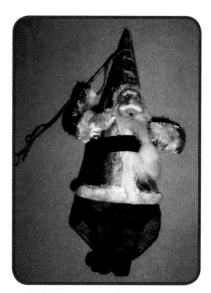

Blue and silver foil Santa, composition and paper.
$75.00 – 95.00.

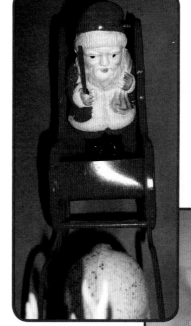

Celluloid Santa and sleigh with two gold-sprinkled
reindeer, 14" long. $150.00 – 250.00.

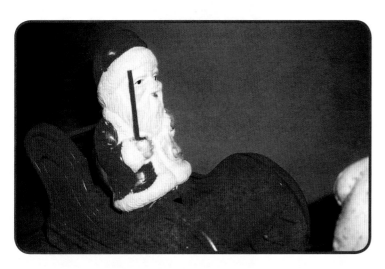

Chenille and composition ornament, 4"
long. $75.00 – 95.00.

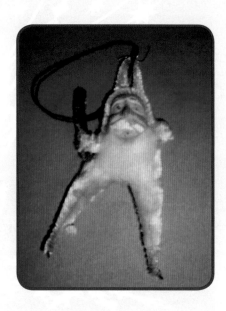

White chenille (pipe cleaner) ornament, 3" long.
$65.00 – 90.00.

Red chenille ornament, 4" long with composition
face. $75.00 – 95.00.

Red chenille and paper bell ornament, early.
$150.00 – 225.00.

Red Santa-face bell ornament with beaded attachments, wool beard. $200.00 – 375.00.

Green chenille ornament, composition face. $65.00 – 95.00.

Cloth and composition ornament with detailed face, wool beard. $150.00 – 200.00.

Large statue, 8", with composition face. $200.00 – 275.00.

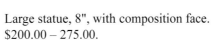

Small cloth and composition figure, 3".
$60.00 – 75.00.

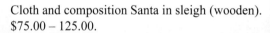

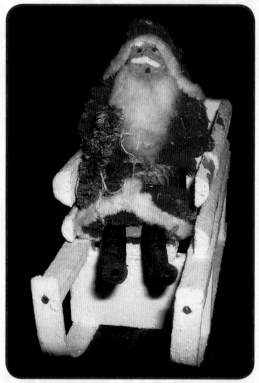

Cloth and composition Santa in sleigh (wooden).
$75.00 – 125.00.

Small composition and cloth figure, 4", with rope
and bag. $110.00 – 180.00.

Cloth doll, 10", with wax face and chenille trimmings, rare. $225.00 – 375.00.

Head-in-stocking decoration, 5". $125.00 – 200.00.

Cloth and celluloid mesh candy container, rare. $175.00 – 250.00.

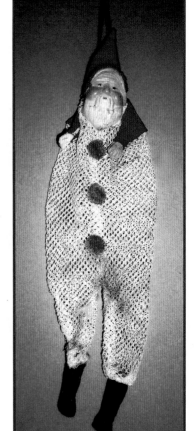

Pot-metal bank, 8". $125.00 – 200.00.

Chalk statue, 10". $150.00 – 225.00.

Different view of preceding statue.

Large celluloid figural rattle, 8".
$200.00 – 300.00.

Rounded celluloid statue, 5". $125.00 – 150.00.

Santa Claus with reindeer and sleigh, 4" long. $75.00 – 125.00.

Unusual celluloid rattle of Santa Claus with two children, rare. $200.00 – 325.00.

Celluloid Santa Claus figure, 5". $145.00 – 200.00.

Celluloid Santa Claus with lantern figure, 4", unusual pose and paint colors. $150.00 – 245.00.

Tall celluloid Santa Claus figure, 8". $210.00 – 275.00.

Celluloid figure, Santa on sleigh pulled by goat or sheep, 4" long. $125.00 – 175.00.

Small celluloid roly-poly, 4" tall. $125.00 – 200.00.

Santa Claus in North Pole housemobile, car/ house combo. Rare. $250.00 – 375.00.

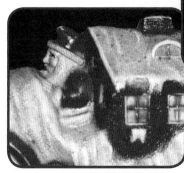

Celluloid rattle, Santa Claus with toys and bag, large 6". $225.00 – 275.00.

Same as above, back view.

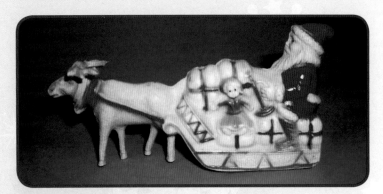

Santa Claus with toys, on sleigh being pulled by goat, celluloid, 5". $200.00 – 250.00.

Celluloid rattle, Santa Claus with basket of fruit, 4". $150.00 – 235.00.

Celluloid figure, small 4". $75.00 – 125.00.

Jolly celluloid figure, 6". $125.00 – 200.00.

Reverse of photo on left, holding doll.

Small celluloid roly-poly, 4" tall.
$125.00 – 200.00.

Small celluloid toy, Santa in sleigh,
3" long. $125.00 – 165.00.

Celluloid figure, 5" tall. $125.00 – 200.00.

Santa in sleigh, all celluloid, 5" long with movable
head. $225.00 –300.00.

Jovial round-faced sprite ornament, composition. $65.00 – 90.00.

Santa on skis and with a pack on his back, composition and wood. $125.00 – 200.00.

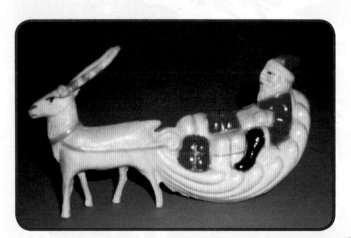

Celluloid figure, Santa on sleigh pulled by a reindeer. $145.00 – 195.00.

Composition, wood, and cloth Santa on skis, 6" tall. $125.00 – 200.00.

Composition Santa and snowman in tiny tree-base house. $75.00 – 125.00.

Composition and celluloid Santa on round base, 7" tall. $135.00 – 200.00.

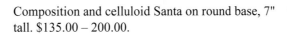

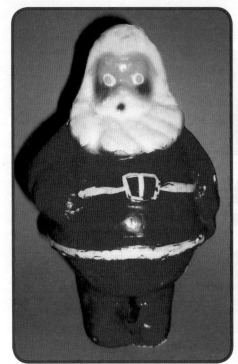

Composition figure, 7" tall. $125.00 – 175.00.

Small composition and cloth Santa with chenille branch. $85.00 – 150.00.

Another version of the preceding item, this is very similar. $85.00 – 150.00.

Small dwarflike candy container. $50.00 – 75.00.

Lot of four hangtag ornaments (paper) from bank promotion. $30.00 – 50.00.

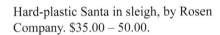

Hard-plastic Santa in sleigh, by Rosen Company. $35.00 – 50.00.

Small Rosen hard-plastic ornament. $20.00 – 30.00.

Early lithographed candy tin. $150.00 – 225.00.

Wooden toy in original box made at Santa Claus, Indiana. $1,200.00 – 1,800.00.

Large composition Santa-head decoration, extremely rare, 22" tall. $750.00 – 1,000.00.

Tall celluloid and cloth doll, 12". $50.00 – 75.00.

Small (4") composition figure. $20.00 – 30.00.

Small bisque figure, 3" tall. $15.00 – 20.00.

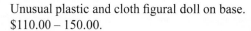
Unusual plastic and cloth figural doll on base. $110.00 – 150.00.

Celluloid and cloth Santa (with girl-like features) doll, on base. $75.00 – 95.00.

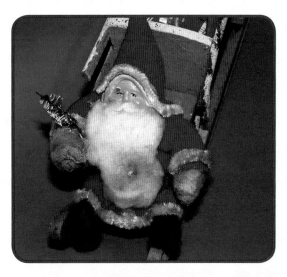

Celluloid and cloth Santa on wooden sleigh (date uncertain). $75.00 – 125.00.

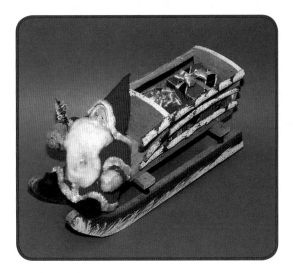

Large and mint early Santa doll with cotton beard, 15". $250.00 – 350.00.

Celluloid Santa Claus and all eight reindeer, complete on base. $150.00 – 250.00.

Cloth and composition Santa Claus jack-in-the-box.
$150.00 – 250.00.

Papier mâché and composition candy
container. $135.00 – 225.00.

Santa Claus (troll-like) figure in green coat.
$75.00 – 125.00.

Figural candy container, 10". $100.00 – 165.00.

Composition Santa in boot, unusual.
$125.00 – 200.00.

Cloth and composition doll on base, with
basket. $125.00 – 155.00.

Older composition and cloth doll, with fur
beard and on base. $225.00 – 295.00.

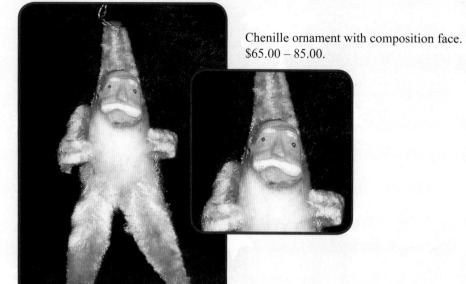

Chenille ornament with composition face.
$65.00 – 85.00.

Figure with wax or celluloid face, 6".
$125.00 – 175.00.

Cast-iron figure on skis, complete with poles,
3" tall. $125.00 – 200.00.

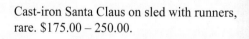

Cast-iron Santa Claus on sled with runners,
rare. $175.00 – 250.00.

Small gnomelike figure with tree,
4". $75.00 – 125.00.

Cast-iron figure, Santa Claus on yellow
sled. $125.00 – 200.00.

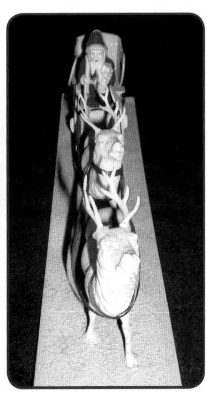

Celluloid Santa Claus and two reindeer set
on permanent base. $135.00 – 200.00.

Large 8" figural light bulb (decorative, works!).
$125.00 – 200.00.

Smaller 5" figural light bulb (also works).
$75.00 – 125.00.

Comparison of two bulbs shown in photos above.

Cookie mold sheet. $65.00 – 100.00.

Composition figure with cotton beard, on base.
$125.00 – 150.00.

Conical-shaped Santa, on base, composition
construction. $75.00 – 95.00.

Composition and cloth Santa, on base, 6".
$125.00 – 145.00.

Composition and cloth Santa with cotton
beard, on base, 5". $135.00 – 165.00.

Pretty-faced doll with girl-like features,
20". $235.00 – 400.00.

Jolly, friendly-faced doll (missing beard), 24".
$250.00 – 395.00.

Santa holding stick or cane, composition and cloth doll. $125.00 – 145.00.

Composition ornament, Santa on skis, intended to hang. $75.00 – 100.00.

Ornament with composition face and cloth body. $75.00 – 100.00.

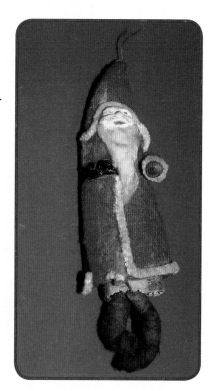

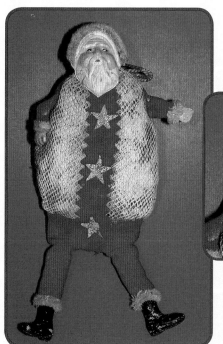

Celluloid and cloth beanbag-type candy holder. $85.00 – 110.00.

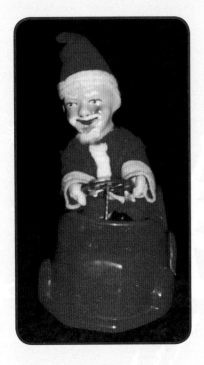

Unusual composition figure in plastic car. $225.00 – 300.00.

Composition statue/doll. $75.00 – 125.00.

Composition figure, 10". $150.00 – 225.00.

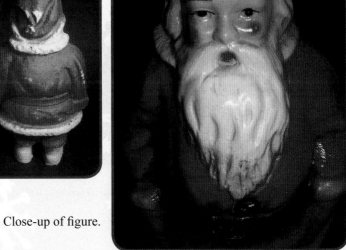

Close-up of figure.

Pressed paper (papier mâché) figure, 10".
$75.00 – 100.00.

Green composition figure, 7".
$85.00 – 150.00.

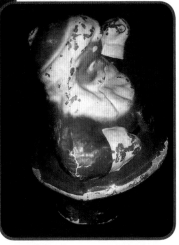

Unusual white-clad paper composition figure.
$125.00 – 175.00.

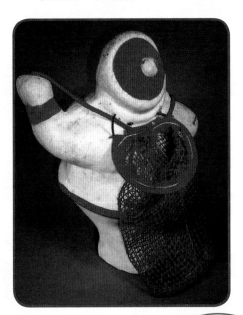

Red 6" composition figure. $65.00 – 100.00.

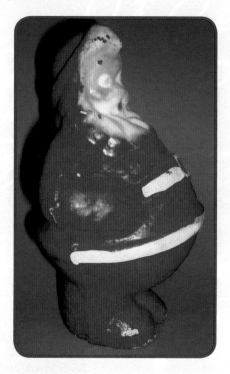

Red 8" composition figure.
$125.00 – 200.00.

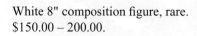

White 8" composition figure, rare.
$150.00 – 200.00.

Extremely rare Santa on Polar Bear figure, composition. $400.00 – 600.00.

Small 5" composition figure. $75.00 – 100.00.

Early Santa doll with childlike face, stuffed
with cloth and straw. $300.00 – 500.00.

Postcard of Kewpie playing Santa, circa 1920, Rose O'Neill. $35.00 – 70.00.

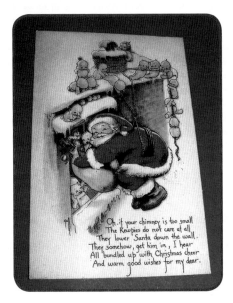

Santa and Kewpies postcard, circa 1920, Rose O'Neill. $35.00 – 70.00.

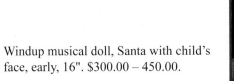

Windup musical doll, Santa with child's face, early, 16". $300.00 – 450.00.

Composition figure, pinecone Santa, on base, 4". $75.00 – 100.00.

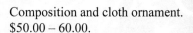
Composition and cloth ornament. $50.00 – 60.00.

Pair of chenille pipe-cleaner ornaments, composition faces. $75.00 – 125.00.

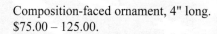
Composition-faced ornament, 4" long. $75.00 – 125.00.

Decoration novelty, Santa on stick, composition face. $50.00 – 75.00.

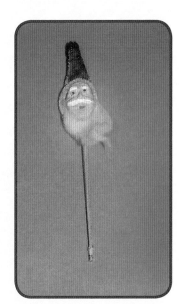

Composition-faced ornament, 4" long. $75.00 – 125.00.

Cloth and composition doll, 7". $125.00 – 175.00.

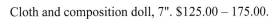

Small composition figure on base. $75.00 – 100.00.

Composition-faced figure holding bag, 4". $65.00 – 95.00.

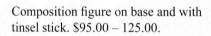

Composition figure on base and with tinsel stick. $95.00 – 125.00.

Small 3" Santa with celluloid face. $50.00 – 75.00.

Older-version Santa with wool beard, on white base, 6". $150.00 – 200.00.

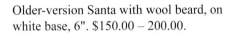

Composition-faced ornament, Santa Claus holding chenille evergreen. $125.00 – 175.00.

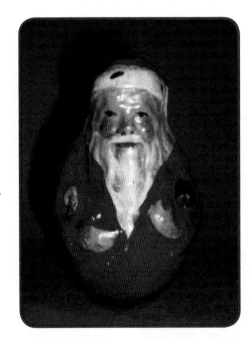

Schoenhut roly-poly figure, rare. $250.00 – 375.00.

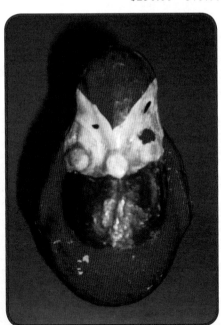

Cloth and composition Santa Claus on skis, 7".
$250.00 – 375.00.

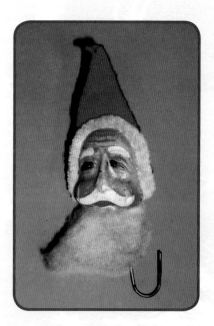

Composition ornament, 4".
$75.00 – 125.00.

Composition-faced ornament, 5".
$125.00 – 175.00.

Hard-plastic ornament. $15.00 – 25.00.

Small bisque Santa Claus and reindeer figure, 4"
long. $50.00 – 75.00.

Small composition figure, 1".
$45.00 – 75.00.

Small bisque figure, 2".
$35.00 – 65.00.

Very small wax or celluloid figure, ¾".
$25.00 – 50.00.

Wool and cloth seated Santa Claus figure. $125.00 – 155.00.

Santa Claus in blue paper and foil and on celluloid reindeer. $135.00 – 195.00.

Composition-faced Santa ornament, with chenille sprig, 3". $75.00 – 100.00.

Santa Claus, with composition face and felt clothes, on base, 5". $150.00 – 195.00.

Same as above, side view.

Composition and cloth figure on base, 4".
$75.00 – 110.00.

Composition-faced cloth ornament, 4".
$95.00 – 125.00.

Figure on white base, 5".
$75.00 – 95.00.

Cookie cutter, old. $30.00 – 50.00.

Figure on base and holding chenille branch, 5". $85.00 – 125.00.

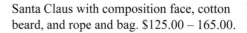

Santa Claus with composition face, cotton beard, and rope and bag. $125.00 – 165.00.

The Night before Christmas book, c. 1917 by the Stecher Litho. Co. $75.00 – 100.00.

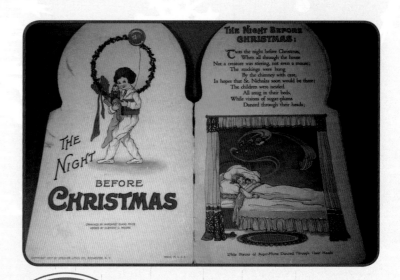

Inside pages of book shown on preceding page.

A Visit to Santa Claus, children's picture book, circa 1920s. $45.00 – 70.00.

Sears Toyland Christmas Santa ad. $35.00 – 70.00.

Santa Claus Big Picture and Story Book.
$75.00 – 95.00.

The Christmas Book, early Santa book, 1930s. $45.00 – 75.00.

Mickey and Minnie Mouse with Santa, lithographed print, large. $75.00 – 100.00.

Package tag, 1930s, 4". $10.00 – 20.00.

The 1940s and the 1950s saw the largest part of the jump in birth rate that began the Baby Boom era. Just following the victory of World War Two and for the two decades immediately following, Americans turned their sights on home, family, and certainly Christmas with a passion! As with the two decades immediately preceding this time, mass availability of Christmas items fueled the marketplace such that Christmas decorations and collectibles appeared on the dime-store shelves just after Halloween, and collectors blew right past Thanksgiving decorations and began to purchase them as soon as the frost was on the pumpkin!

Collectors today can find loads of treasures packed away in Christmas storage boxes. Certainly the most frequently found items are the standard Christmas tree ornaments of the period, but the smart 1940s and 1950s homemaker knew that decorating for the holidays now meant much more that putting up a Christmas tree on Christmas Eve.

Consider my own family background. My mother was born in 1925 and lived in an urban setting in Indiana. Her family practiced as tradition what most families of that era observed — the Christmas celebration lasted just a day or two. On Christmas Eve, my grandfather would head to a local woods, find a tree, and chop it down, and it stayed in the house for maybe two or three days. Its glorious display really lasted only about 30 hours, from Christmas Eve at sundown until the morning of December 26. Consequently, my mother (now 83) has no childhood memories of any family Christmas decorations being displayed other than the ornaments on the Christmas tree.

Now, fast forward one entire generation and consider my own childhood. I was born in 1954, and although my mother continually tried to restrain me from beginning Christmas before Thanksgiving was over, we had a long mantle over our staircase that began sporting Christmas figural wax candles and celluloid plastic figurines (thanks to me!) a day or two after Halloween. Although my mom and dad complained, I don't think they minded the early holiday decoration intrusion. The point to be made here is that the Baby Boomer generation generally celebrated a much longer Christmas season than most of their parents did just a couple of decades earlier. One factor that played into this scenario is that, in general, American affluence increased and families had more disposable income to use for holiday decorating. Another factor is that the virtual explosion of the family dime-store chain now placed an S.S. Kresge, W.T. Grant, Woolworth's, or any of a dozen other similar stores in the town square of even the smallest rural town, so now everybody had complete access to Christmas (and Santa) holiday decorations and inexpensive trinkets. It was time to get the storage boxes ready, because now we could fill them!

Figures made in Japan of glazed ceramic or china became popular holiday decorating staples during the 1940s and 1950s. These figures were very inexpensive. Most families had at least a small collection, because if the figures were packed away well, they were quite sturdy and lasted for years. The colors on these examples are amazing, and the shine drives even the youngest hands to want to pick them up, examine them, and explore their slick, smooth, shiny beauty. Simply put, they are exquisite to both look at and touch.

The decades of the 1920s and the 1930s saw celluloid toys and figurines working their way into holiday designs, so if those decades could be coined the celluloid years, then the 1940s through the 1960s would have to be known as the age of plastic. We are not talking the pliable, rubbery, squishy vinyls that are used for dog toys and children's playpen squeakers of today; this era brought us the highly attractive sturdy, durable, slick hard plastics. These toys have a strong structure generally, but because this early plastic is quite brittle, collectors should be on guard to make sure examples of these holiday collectibles aren't missing ears, legs, fingers, noses, or other appendages or trim. Two of the most prolific of the plastic manufacturing companies dealing in hard plastic Christmas and Santa display collectibles were the E. Rosen Company and Irwin Plastics. Both companies supplied dime-store shelves with brightly colored hard plastic candy containers, light-up figural Christmas decorations, figurines, rolling Santa toys, and Christmas novelty decorations.

Santa collectibles from these decades also exhibit a sort of modernization of the character. As the 1950s gave witness to the rise of interest in science fiction, the advent of the space race, and more frequent sightings of U.F.O.s, American tastes began to shift toward a modernization of both line and function in furniture, low-profile ranch houses, automobiles with jet-engine-looking fins and cockpit-styled dashboards, and a Santa Claus who had a more updated look. Certainly Santa still sported the same bright red clothes and had a fluffy beard, but the Santa Claus toys, decorations, and figurines of the 1950s through the 1960s show a Santa who is evolving into more of a rounded, stereotypical, almost cartoonlike TV character and looks less like the Victorian or nostalgic-looking old-fashioned Santa of previous generations. In essence, he is depicted as a sharper Santa Claus with a cleaner visible line.

A case in point is the Haddon Sundblom Santa, depicted in the 1940s through the 1960s in

Coca-Cola ads. Sundblom's rendition of St. Nick would change the way we viewed our beloved character; most importantly, after his redesign of Santa, it was hard to picture him without a bottle of Coca-Cola in his hand! Although at the outset he would appear to be an old-fashioned Santa, in truth, even the Sundlbom Santa is modern in design. His graphic image is rather clean and simple. This new personage created by Sundblom's designs begged to be displayed on billboards and mass marketed in other ways. Thus, Coca-Cola, with a two-decade-long ad campaign, forever changed the way we looked at Santa. The plush collector Santa dolls marketed by the Rushton Company in the 1950s, and the more recent versions re-released in the 1980s and 1990s, all did their part to keep the association of Santa with Coca-Cola products alive for generations to come. Collectors should check the copyright dates stamped on these Santa dolls to date them; it is very hard to gauge the age of a Rushton-produced doll without checking the copyright information first. Generally, the best indicator is condition. Although newer plush Santa dolls that are dirty or soiled can have an old look, it is impossible to age or duplicate the aging process on a doll whose plastic/vinyl face has the aged look of a doll exposed to light and the elements

for 40 or 50 years. Check the condition, and check the copyright information. Even most newer releases of the Rushton Santas are worth over $100, but a truly vintage 1950s doll in near-mint condition can be worth three to four times that amount. (See the pictures in both this and the next chapter.)

The Santa collectibles of this time period are those that are dearest to this author's heart, because they are from my own childhood. Each collector must decide for himself or herself where his or her own special preferences lie, but generally, it is the Santas that we grew up with that are the ones we treasure most. The intention of each of the chapters in this book is to give both the casual and the advanced collector an idea of what was produced during each era.

Baby Boomers truly had their own special Santa. He's the Santa depicted in the now-classic film *A Christmas Story,* a Santa who sits high atop the scenic display in the local department store, a display complete with slide or pretty elves in short dresses or Candy Cane Land or whatever theme the store owner decided to work with. It was in this fun environment that our own images of Santa Claus were permanently established, and from these first meetings, many of us became permanent Santa collectors!

Plastic doll, 12". $75.00 – 125.00.

Large plastic doll with gold foil trim. $65.00 – 100.00.

Large composition and cloth doll, 10".
$125.00 – 200.00.

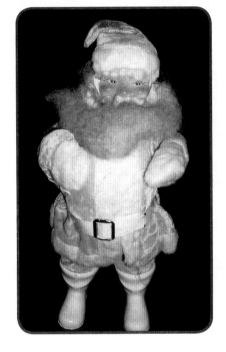

Cloth and composition doll dressed in
pink, 14". $130.00 – 190.00.

Santa Claus in white velvet suit, composition,
with wool beard, 12". $125.00 – 200.00.

White and African-American versions of Santa
Claus. $65.00 – 100.00 each.

Fat and jolly doll with wool beard, 10".
$135.00 – 165.00.

Santa Claus with red beard and dressed like
Disney dwarf, unusual. $75.00 – 100.00.

Cloth and composition doll with movable head,
by Gund. $150.00 – 225.00.

Composition Mr. and Mrs. Santa Claus dolls.
$200.00 – 300.00 for pair.

Vinyl and plastic doll, green version, 14".
$75.00 – 135.00.

Vinyl doll, with straight beard, plush, 14".
$75.00 – 135.00.

Cloth and vinyl doll, plush beard. $75.00 – 125.00.

Cloth and vinyl doll, pink version, soft plush beard. $85.00 – 135.00.

Doll with fur-type plush beard, light green cloth. $85.00 – 135.00.

Vinyl and plush doll, all original. $125.00 – 200.00.

Vinyl and plush doll, black version, rare. $150.00 – 250.00.

Plastic and composition doll. $125.00 – 165.00.

Figural candy container. $75.00 – 95.00.

Glitter-flocked candy container, faux-fur beard. $65.00 – 95.00.

Composition candy container, cotton beard. $75.00 – 100.00.

Bisque statue. $75.00 – 95.00.

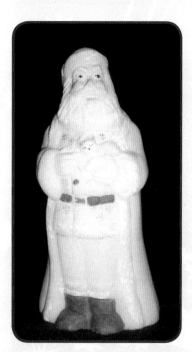

Bisque statue, white and blue version. $85.00 – 110.00.

Vinyl or rubber squeak figure by Sunnyslope, 8". $75.00 – 125.00.

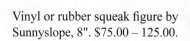

African American doll holding Coca-Cola bottle. $75.00 – 110.00.

Plush doll with silver/white cloth body. $125.00 – 165.00.

Candy container, 8". $75.00 – 100.00.

Decoration figure, plastic.
$50.00 – 75.00.

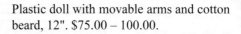

Plastic doll with movable arms and cotton beard, 12". $75.00 – 100.00.

Close-up of doll above.

Squeak toy, soft rubber, 10". $35.00 – 75.00.

Very ornate jewelry-store display figure, 12". $200.00 – 300.00.

Doll with plastic face and cloth body, 12". $75.00 – 125.00.

Ornate doll with fluffy wool beard, 12". $150.00 – 225.00.

Cloth, plastic, and tin windup toy, bell ringer. $100.00 – 145.00.

Plush doll, 1950s, mint. $150.00 – 225.00.

Wooden push puppet with bag.
$75.00 – 95.00.

Hand puppet with rubber or vinyl head. $45.00 – 75.00.

Child's doll, cloth face. $75.00 – 100.00.

Chenille fabric dolls. $65.00 – 90.00.

Chenille fabric doll close-up.

Composition rocking figure, 8" tall.
$125.00 – 200.00.

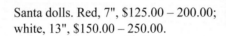
Santa dolls. Red, 7", $125.00 – 200.00;
white, 13", $150.00 – 250.00.

Small plastic doll, 8".
$65.00 – 90.00.

Cloth and vinyl doll, 10". $70.00 – 90.00.

Cloth and vinyl doll, with cotton beard.
$125.00 – 150.00.

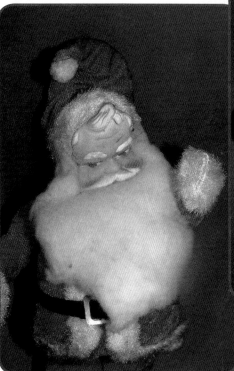

Satin doll, plastic face, 24" tall. $225.00 – 300.00.

Plush cloth doll with vinyl face.
$75.00 – 125.00.

Battery-operated mechanical
toy. $150.00 – 225.00.

Tin windup, Santa Claus on tricycle, with
celluloid balloon, Japan. $125.00 – 175.00.

Windup Santa Claus drummer, with fur beard.
$75.00 – 100.00.

Tin windup bell ringer. $125.00 – 200.00.

Whistle toy by the E. Rosen Company, with original candy. $100.00 – 200.00.

Santa Claus with reindeer pull toy, by the E. Rosen Company. $125.00 – 250.00.

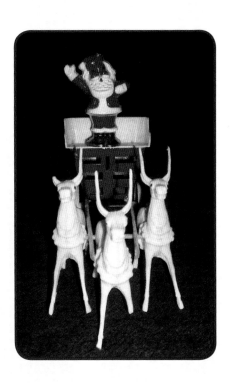

Pull toy/decoration by the E. Rosen Company. $125.00 – 225.00.

Creamer set, three pieces, ceramic. $100.00 – 150.00.

Three different versions of an E. Rosen Santa on a reindeer. $75.00 – 100.00 each.

E. Rosen Santa on brown reindeer. $75.00 – 100.00.

E. Rosen Santa on white reindeer. $75.00 – 100.00.

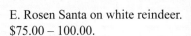

E. Rosen Santa Claus on darker brown reindeer.
$75.00 – 100.00.

E. Rosen decoration Santa holding
packages. $50.00 – 65.00.

Santa Claus jack-in-the-box figure. $50.00 – 65.00.

Plastic Santa Claus jack-in-the-box figure.
$45.00 – 65.00.

Plastic candy containers, push-up surprise Santa Clauses. $40.00 – 60.00 each.

Different view of one of a push-up surprise Santas shown above.

Different view of one of the Santas shown above.

Plastic jack-in-the-box toy, Santa Claus in boot. $65.00 – 95.00.

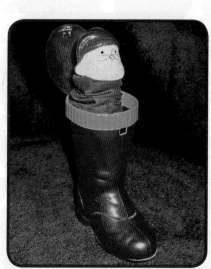

Santa Claus jack-in-the-box by Fun World, made in Hong Kong. $35.00 – 60.00.

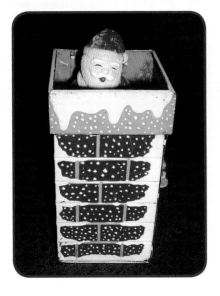

Santa Claus in chimney action toy, cardboard and plastic. $65.00 – 90.00.

Santa Claus jack-in-the-box in original, hard-to-find box. $100.00 – 135.00.

Santa Claus jack-in-the-box toy of preceding set.

Close-up of the same set.

Plastic and cardboard push-up toy, Santa Claus with cotton beard. $75.00 – 90.00.

Santa Claus in chimney toy, shown with original box. $75.00 – 95.00.

Battery-operated Santa Claus bell ringer, with plastic face, 12" tall. $110.00 – 140.00.

Battery-operated Santa Claus bell-ringer bank toy in original box. $100.00 – 150.00.

Plastic Santa Claus and reindeer display set with box. $75.00 – 110.00.

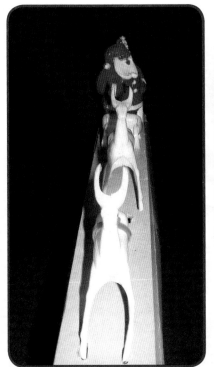

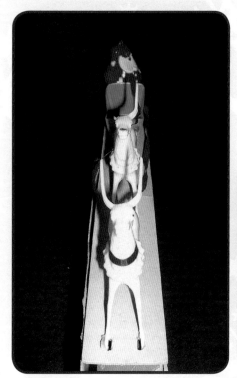

Plastic Santa Claus and reindeer display set with box. $75.00 – 110.00.

Plastic Santa Claus and reindeer display set with box, by Irwin. $85.00 – 135.00.

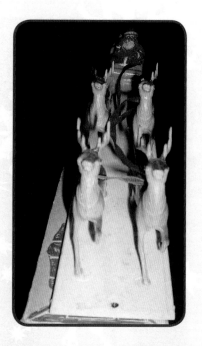

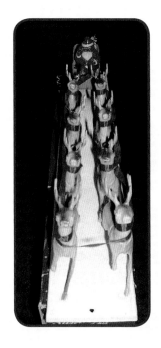

Plastic display set by Irwin, Santa Claus with eight reindeer. $100.00 – 150.00.

Plastic mantel display, Santa Claus and reindeer, with box. $75.00 – 95.00.

Santa Claus on reindeer, early Rosen plastic figure. $75.00 – 100.00.

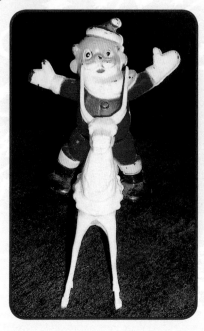

Santa Claus in plastic sleigh with single reindeer. $45.00 – 65.00.

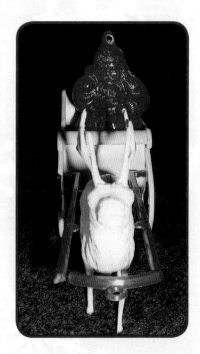

Boxed mantel set, Santa Claus and two reindeer.
$75.00 – 100.00.

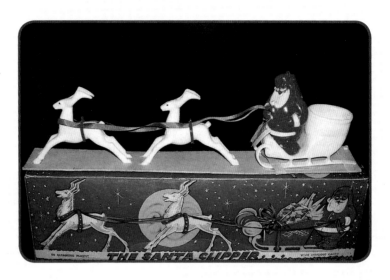

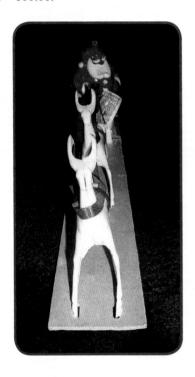

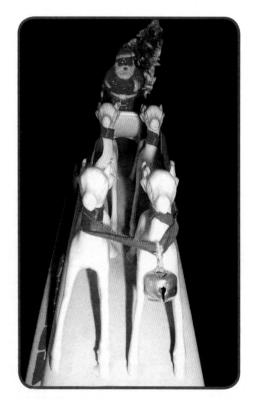

Boxed mantel set by Irwin, Santa Claus and four
reindeer. $100.00 – 135.00.

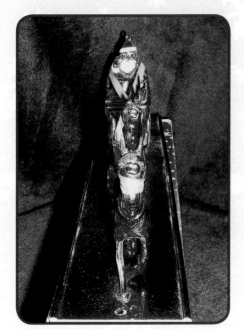

Santa Claus and His Reindeer boxed mantel set, red metallic plastic. $100.00 – 125.00.

Mrs. Santa Claus plastic toothbrush holder. $40.00 – 65.00.

Hard-plastic push puppet, great action toy.
$25.00 – 40.00.

Tin windup action toy, with bell-ringing
action. $75.00 – 125.00.

Tin windup toy, Santa Claus on skis, with
plastic head. $75.00 – 95.00.

Windup toy, Santa Claus bell ringer holding big white bag, with plastic face. $75.00 – 110.00.

Tin windup, Santa Claus with plastic face and cloth body, on lithographed base. $110.00 – 140.00.

Santa Claus bell-ringer windup toy holding pipe-cleaner candy cane. $75.00 – 90.00.

Santa Claus reading book, page-turning windup toy, by Alps of Japan. $110.00 – 140.00.

Mantle set, Santa Claus and six reindeer, probably by Irwin. $80.00 – 120.00.

Plastic Santa Claus figure on skis, 6". $45.00 – 60.00.

Small plastic waving Santa Claus. $20.00 – 30.00.

Small plastic Santa Claus holding Christmas pine. $15.00 – 30.00.

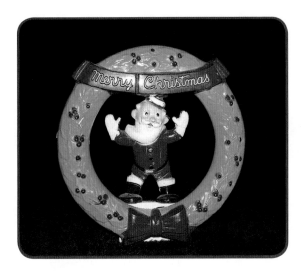

Plastic Santa wreath "Merry Christmas" decoration by E. Rosen. $45.00 – 75.00.

Light-up Santa wreath decoration by Miller Co., in original box. $125.00 – 150.00.

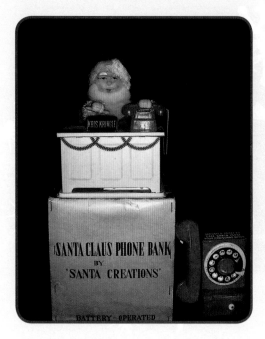

Battery-operated phone bank by Santa Creations, in box. $125.00 – 200.00.

Windup toy, Santa Claus riding a tricycle, Japan, 1950s. $125.00 – 175.00.

Battery-operated bell-ringing toy. $125.00 – 150.00.

Small plastic ornament. $10.00 – 15.00.

Small plastic Santa by Irwin, 1950s. $20.00 – 30.00.

Tin windup toy, Santa Claus bell ringer, 1960s.
$125.00 – 200.00.

Battery-operated bell ringer in original box with tags. $135.00 – 225.00.

Celluloid windup bell ringer, Santa Claus on sleigh, with box. $150.00 – 245.00.

Plastic push-up puppet, 5" tall. $20.00 – 35.00.

Tin and plastic windup, Santa Claus on tricycle. $65.00 – 90.00.

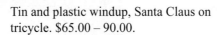

Irwin Plastics Corp. decoration, Santa in sleigh. $25.00 – 45.00.

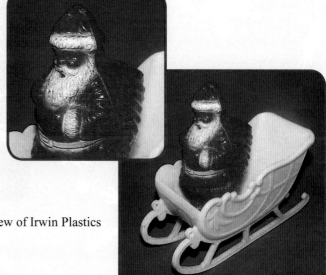

Close-up and different view of Irwin Plastics Corp. Santa.

Irwin Plastics ornament. $15.00 – 20.00.

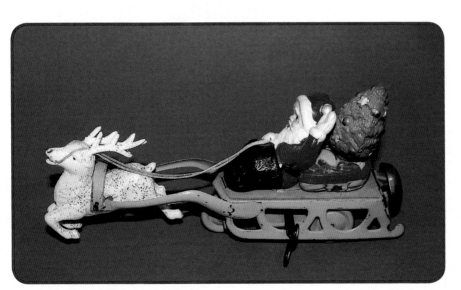

Celluloid windup, Santa Claus pulled by reindeer, bell ringer. $125.00 – 225.00.

Hard-plastic night-light. $20.00 – 40.00.

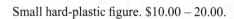

Small hard-plastic figure. $10.00 – 20.00.

Hard-plastic figurine, detailed face. $30.00 – 45.00.

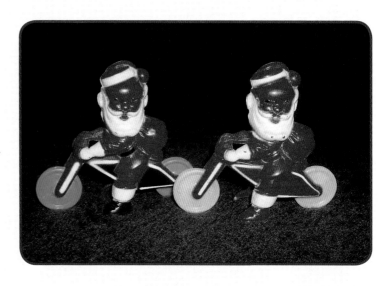

Hard-plastic figures on bicycles. $45.00 – 65.00 each.

Plastic ornament with tag/card. $25.00 – 40.00.

Hard-plastic ornaments with tools, set of five. $200.00 – 250.00.

Santa riding in old-time automobile, hard-plastic toy. $125.00 – 155.00.

Composition nodder figure, with short beard style. $125.00 – 175.00.

Tin lithographed clicker toy, Japan. $5.00 – 10.00.

Glass Santa Claus figural piece.
$35.00 – 65.00.

Cartoonlike tin windup, Santa and funny
reindeer, 12". $125.00 – 200.00.

Battery-operated Happy Santa drummer, in
original box. $125.00 – 200.00.

Ceramic Santa and ballerina figurine combination, 7". $75.00 – 95.00.

Bank, spaghetti-type hat trim, 8". $65.00 – 100.00.

Pitcher and cups set, ceramic, 1950s.
$125.00 – 200.00.

Large chalk bank, Santa writing list, 12".
$125.00 – 150.00.

Painted ceramic planter, 7" long.
$65.00 – 100.00.

Pot-metal bank, 8". $75.00 – 125.00.

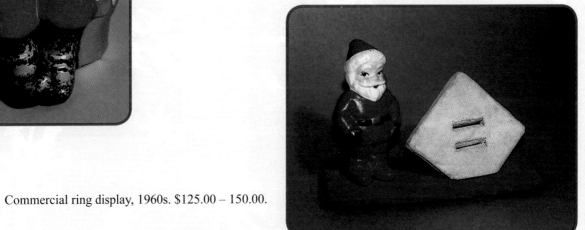

Commercial ring display, 1960s. $125.00 – 150.00.

Giant chalk figure, very colorful, 14" tall.
$75.00 – 95.00.

Ceramic planter by Leeds, Mickey Mouse as Santa
Claus. $75.00 – 100.00.

Pot-metal bank, 8". $75.00 – 125.00.

Citizens Fidelity premium pot-metal Santa Claus bank, 6".
$75.00 – 100.00.

Large wax candle, 7". $35.00 – 50.00.

Large wax candle, 5". $35.00 – 50.00.

Light-up Santa Claus face, 1960s. $40.00 – 60.00.

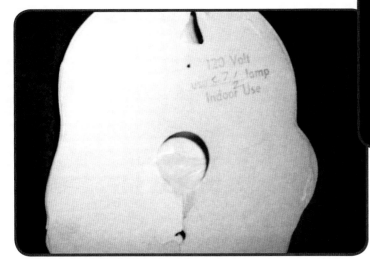

Light-up door decoration, 1960s. $60.00 – 80.00.

Light-up Santa Claus and Howdy Doody door decoration. $145.00 – 210.00.

Light-up decoration, Santa Claus with bag of toys, 26". $150.00 – 195.00.

Light-up wall decoration, plastic, 20". $110.00 – 150.00.

Hard-plastic light-up wall decoration, 24". $75.00 – 125.00.

Decorative container with lithographed print. $35.00 – 55.00.

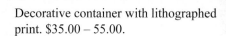

Lithographed Mrs. Steven's Santa Claus candy tin. $40.00 – 65.00.

Lithographed Santa Claus cookie/candy tin.
$35.00 – 45.00.

Decorated box of Christmas cards.
$25.00 – 40.00.

Vintage Coca-Cola cardboard store
display, 20" tall. $175.00 – 300.00.

Cardboard hanging ornament.
$10.00 – 20.00.

Lithographed 1960s cardboard candy box.
$20.00 – 35.00.

Vintage paper Coca-Cola ad. $25.00 – 50.00.

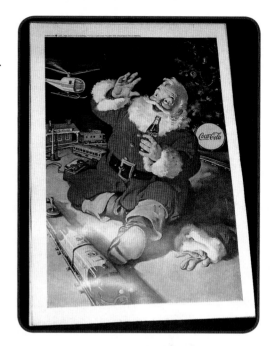

Almost life-sized heavy cardboard store display. $350.00 – 500.00.

Life-sized Coca-Cola cardboard store display. $300.00 – 450.00.

This book has already taken the reader on a whirlwind tour of some 80 years of Santa Claus collectibles. By now, the reader is aware that there are literally hundreds of possibilities for Santa collecting specialties, with thousands of specimens spread out over nearly a hundred years. But I would be remiss if an attempt was not made to at least introduce the novice collector to what items from the recent past and currently on the market are worthy of being collected for posterity.

Beginning in the early 1970s, limited editioning became a common practice among collecting companies. Driven by the popularity of such companies as both the Franklin Mint and the Danbury Mint, companies began to realize there was a strong market among collectors for collectible items that were only available for a limited time, or in relatively limited supply. Consequently, many Santa figures and dolls have been manufactured and marketed over the past 30 years with limited-edition practices. Depending upon the design of the product, and also depending on actual integrity of the limited-edition process, collectors may or may not want to recognize this as a suitable way to establish value in a future collectible. My take on this has always been that if the edition size is actually limited to less than the scope of the demand, then you will have a collectible that may appreciate over time. Unfortunately, marketing methods have improved in recent years, so if an edition of Santas or dolls is limited to only 5,000 pieces, it may be a pretty good bet that there are probably less than 5,000 collectors who actually want that particular example. My advice: Don't use limited-edition status as the only consideration when anticipating whether a piece will increase in value. For value to accrue and appreciate, there has to be a future demand for an item, and it is very difficult to determine what modern collectibles of today will be valuable and desired tomorrow, especially when it comes to a subject so endearing as Santa Claus.

The best advice for collecting Santas from the modern era is to buy what you like and what displays nicely in your home with all of your other Santas. If you are a true lover of that which is antique or very old, then stick with buying what you prefer. It is a given fact that antiques appreciate at a more rapid rate than recent collectibles, so if monetary considerations are important, invest in true antique and collectible Santas from the past. But if simply displaying objects as art or nostalgia pieces are your only considerations, then purchasing reproductions or recent limited editions isn't a bad practice. The latter is easier on your wallet; the former is better for investment.

There is a plethora of modern Santa art, toys, figures, and collectibles for the buyer to purchase. Aside from the financial limitations on just buying everything out there, remember that for three fourths of the year, you have to put it away and store it. This collector's advice is to buy only what really strikes you on a personal level, and if you want Santas for investment purposes, skip recent limited editions or newer designer items and go back, way back, to the earliest Santas. Now that these are over 100 years removed from the original general store shelves where they were first purchased, they have rarity and value. You can never go wrong with true rarities. But, that's just my advice. The fact that you purchased this book means that you are in some way intrigued by Christmas and Santa collecting and you want to know more about it.

It is this author's hope that our whirlwind tour of nearly 600 objects representing some 120 years of Santa history and production has in some way helped you to decide what it is you really love about Santa Claus. If you are still deciding, then it is this author's hope that this book will help you make some decisions.

Happy Santa collecting in the days ahead. Remember, every day is Christmas for a Santa collector!

Recent Santa Claus resin figure.
$55.00 – 85.00.

Recent resin figure with dove and staff. $60.00 – 80.00.

Steiff doll, recent, with Coca-Cola bottle, Steiff tag. $150.00 – 200.00.

Coca-Cola Collectible figure, "Trust Is a Friend." $50.00 – 75.00.

Coca-Cola Collectible figure, "Santa's Delight." $50.00 – 75.00.

Coca-Cola Collectible figure, "The Pause That Refreshes." $50.00 – 75.00.

Coca-Cola Collectible figure, "Santa's Gifts." $50.00 – 75.00.

Coca-Cola ornament, "Christmas Is Love." $35.00 – 45.00.

Resin Coca-Cola collector's plate. $35.00 – 45.00.

Reproduction tin lithographed tray, recent.
$25.00 – 45.00.

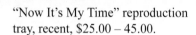

"Now It's My Time" reproduction
tray, recent, $25.00 – 45.00.

Collector's tray, Santa Claus with children,
reproduction. $35.00 – 55.00.

Coca-Cola "Happy Holidays" tray,
reproduction. $25.00 – 45.00.

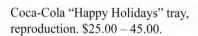

75th Anniversary multiscene Coca-Cola tray. $45.00 – 65.00.

Reproduction collector's tray, Santa with young child. $25.00 – 45.00.

Reproduction tin lithographed tray, "Wherever I Go." $25.00 – 45.00.

Reproduction tin tray, Santa with children and dog. $25.00 – 45.00.

Tin lithographed reproduction tray, oval, old Santa. $25.00 – 45.00.

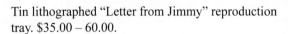

Tin lithographed "Letter from Jimmy" reproduction tray. $35.00 – 60.00.

"Season's Greetings" tin lithographed reproduction tray. $35.00 – 55.00.

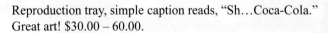

Reproduction tray, simple caption reads, "Sh...Coca-Cola." Great art! $30.00 – 60.00.

Needlepoint-style pillow, nostalgic design.
$35.00 – 50.00.

Coca-Cola special-edition bottle with plastic-wrapped
label, recent. $5.00 – 10.00.

Santa in car, with drive-in tray of Coke and Coke
in his bag, resin figure. $25.00 – 40.00.

Coca-Cola plastic truck with lithographed ads on sides, recent. $15.00 – 25.00.

Coca-Cola December 24 music box, recent. $30.00 – 40.00.

Coca-Cola lithographed cookie tin, recent. $10.00 – 15.00.

Old-time lithographed car bank, recent reproduction. $20.00 – 30.00.

Coca-Cola diecast truck with great old-looking bottles, recent. $25.00 – 40.00.

Plastic collector's car with little elves, recent. $20.00 – 30.00.

Recent snow globe, with "Sh…" scene inside. $25.00 – 35.00.

Santa Claus with black poodle, salt and pepper shakers, recent. $25.00 – 35.00.

Santa Claus resting with a Coke, large ceramic cookie jar, recent. $120.00 – 145.00.

Santa Claus inside snow globe with Coke and toys, recent. $25.00 – 35.00.

Lithographed cookie tin, recent. $8.00 – 15.00.

Resin nodder figure on bottle cap. $35.00 – 45.00.

Collectible Coca-Cola can, recent. $3.00 – 5.00.

Coca-Cola doll, vinyl face, plush beard. $85.00 – 135.00.

Coca-Cola doll, similar version. $75.00 – 125.00.

Coca-Cola doll, plush beard. $85.00 – 135.00.

Santa Claus with outstretched Coke bottle, mint. $100.00 – 145.00.

African-American version, with Coke bottle, recent. $120.00 – 165.00.

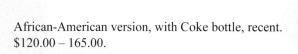

Doll marketed by Gund and copyrighted 1972 and 1988 by Dakin. $100.00 – 150.00.

Small plastic windup figure, recent. $5.00 – 10.00.

Resin ornament on holder, by Holiday Elegance, recent. $20.00 – 35.00.

Celluloid-looking doll on cast-iron holly sled, recent reproduction. $25.00 – 40.00.

Bishop-style cloth St. Nicholas, probably recent, looks old. $35.00 – 50.00.

Reproduction flocked figure, good likeness, 6".
$15.00 – 25.00.

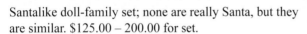

Santalike doll-family set; none are really Santa, but they
are similar. $125.00 – 200.00 for set.

Hand-painted star-shaped novelty box,
recent. $20.00 – 30.00.

Hand-painted star-shaped box, with Santa in relief.
$25.00 – 35.00.

Bisque porcelain figure by Fenton, in box.
$100.00 – 145.00.

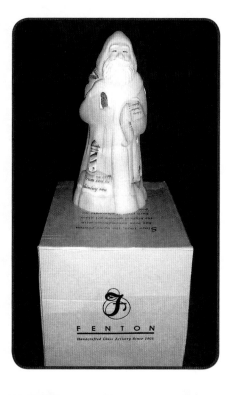

Pair of Fenton figural pieces.
$150.00 – 220.00 for pair.

Pair of Fenton fine glass collectible statues. $125.00 – 225.00
for pair.

Fenton fine glass figure.
$75.00 – 125.00.

Fenton fine glass non-traditional Santa head.
$65.00 – 110.00.

Set of three different Fenton fine glassware
figures in box. $150.00 – 275.00 for set.

Excellent-quality reproduction figure, recent, 10". $20.00 – 30.00.

Resin collectible figure, recent. $65.00 – 120.00.

Santa Claus in chimney reproduction piece, excellent. $20.00 – 30.00.

Beaded figural ornament, recent reproduction. $8.00 – 12.00.

Modern windup action toy, Santa with gears.
$15.00 – 25.00.

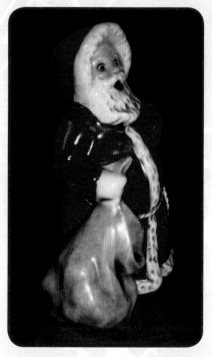

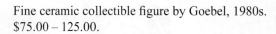
Fine ceramic collectible figure by Goebel, 1980s.
$75.00 – 125.00.

Large figural ornament, recent
reproduction. $10.00 – 12.00.

Excellent reproduction of a vintage figural Belsnickle. $35.00 – 70.00.

Santa kneeling at manger, recent. $25.00 – 40.00.

Fine china statue, excellent quality, 12". $75.00 – 125.00.

Reproduction early Victorian figure, subtle detailing. $25.00 – 40.00.

Glazed ceramic figure, fine china, 8".
$65.00 – 95.00.

Troll-like Santa Claus character in
plaid coat. $75.00 – 95.00.

Decorative item, artist design. $75.00 – 95.00.

Designer container with artist's signature. $75.00 – 125.00.

Figural piece. $75.00 – 110.00.

Figural piece. $75.00 – 110.00.

Figural piece. $75.00 – 110.00.

Large Santa with bag and presents.
$75.00 – 95.00.

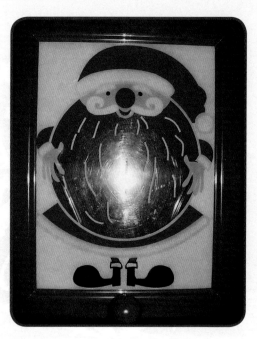

Glass figural art in frame.
$45.00 – 75.00.

Cloth-dressed doll on doll stand.
$65.00 – 80.00.

Santa Murano Italy glass ornament.
$75.00 – 95.00.

Primitive art/craft figure, recent.
$35.00 – 55.00.

Novelty can that serves as a mix-up
puzzle. $25.00 – 45.00.

Novelty can shown on preceding page, in different picture combinations.

Outdoor light-up decoration, recent.
$10.00 – 20.00.

Steiff doll with original tag.
$125.00 – 200.00.

Pullan doll in original box.
$125.00 – 225.00.

Steiff Santa with button and tag.
$135.00 – 210.00.

Steiff doll with button and tag. $130.00 – 200.00.

Steiff hand puppet with tag. $135.00 – 210.00.

Older Steiff Santa Claus, jointed. $145.00 – 235.00.

Recent Steiff Santa Claus with button and tags. $125.00 – 195.00.

Bright gold-plated figure, Japan.
$55.00 – 80.00.

Furry folk-type doll with plastic face, recent.
$75.00 – 110.00.

Thomas Museum series jack-in-the-box. $65.00 – 110.00.

Wooden toy, abstract figural, smiling face. $25.00 – 35.00.

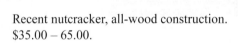
Recent nutcracker, all-wood construction. $35.00 – 65.00.

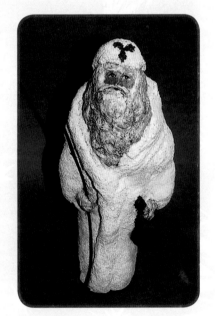

Resin or composition reproduction figure. $25.00 – 40.00.

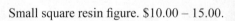
Small square resin figure. $10.00 – 15.00.

Resin candle holder, recent. $15.00 – 25.00.

Reproduction carved-looking figure, recent.
$20.00 – 25.00.

Collectible figure, Santa Claus kneeling at
manger, recent. $65.00 – 95.00.

Blue nutcracker, recent. $65.00 – 100.00.

Red nutcracker, recent. $65.00 – 100.00.

Red carved-type reproduction folk figure. $20.00 – 30.00.

Reproduction Santa marked "1880" but much more recent, iron. $20.00 – 35.00.

Reproduction folk piece. $15.00 – 25.00.

Wood or composition piece, looks like cast iron, recent. $20.00 – 30.00.

Pair of Santas, Godiva chocolates in foil wrap, recent. $20.00 – 30.00 for pair.

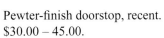

Pewter-finish doorstop, recent. $30.00 – 45.00.

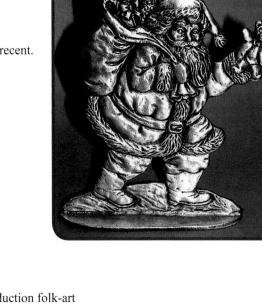

Santa dressed in blue, reproduction folk-art piece. $10.00 – 25.00.

Furry ornament, vintage-style reproduction, hangs. $10.00 – 20.00.

Unusual resin figure, patriotic, with American flag. $20.00 – 35.00.

Mexican-style figure, wood, folk piece. $75.00 – 110.00.

Small plastic rolling toy. $10.00 – 15.00.

Small plastic roly-poly, recent.
$10.00 – 15.00.

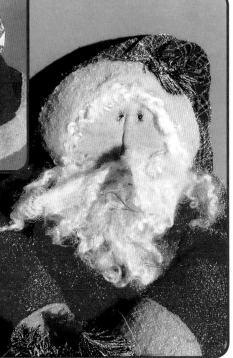

Reproduction folk doll, 20", cloth.
$45.00 – 65.00.

Reproduction antique-style resin figure, 12".
$40.00 – 60.00.

Plaster/resin statue, 10" reproduction. $15.00 – 30.00.

Recent all-wood nutcracker figure, 14". $55.00 – 75.00.

Nutcracker, recent. $50.00 – 75.00.

Folk-style nutcracker, recent.
$40.00 – 70.00.

Recent nutcracker, all wood, unusual design.
$35.00 – 70.00.

Designer hand-blown glass ornament.
$45.00 – 75.00.

Nestled in the rural, rolling hillside country outback of Southern Indiana is a town with a name unlike any others. It could probably better have been served with a name like Lincoln, or Hanks (after the president's mother), because this Spencer County countryside boasts the boyhood trails of young Abe Lincoln. But in the 1840s when the town was established, Abe hadn't made his claim to fame yet. So the Lincoln name wasn't considered, even though Lincoln had lived nearby. Paul Harvey, the national radio commentator, immortalized the town with the history of its name on Christmas Eve, 1992, exactly 140 years after the night the town was named.

That should give readers a clue as to its origins. But the story goes back a decade earlier. It seems that the majority of German immigrants who founded and populated those early hillsides had enough to do just working a living out of the hilly, knobby, and rolling farmland. Picking out a suitable name escaped them for some 12 years after the unofficial 1840 founding. Most visitors and passersby just called it "that nameless town," and everyone knew they were referring to the little hamlet in Southern Indiana.

Well, according to legend, the town fathers, mothers, and children gathered in the local church on Christmas Eve, 1852. They were determined to name the town that night, or no one would leave. It was sort of a forced deadline situation, and everyone wanted to be home before Christmas morning. Some offered to name the town after the local minister, but he declined. As the story goes, a hefty Southern Indiana wind rustled up and blew the church door wide open — and all the little ones in the church turned around and squealed, believing they heard sleigh bells outside in the blowing snowflakes, and they shouted, "It's Santa Claus! It's Santa Claus!" To the adults inside, the kids had come up with the town name in short order. Others heard the sleigh bells that night as well, and as it was 1852, there indeed could have been a passing sleigh. But Spencer County is remote, and everyone who lived there was in the church. But there were those bells, and the wind. And the door. And forever thereafter, the town became known as "Santa Claus."

With such inspired origins, it is no wonder that little Santa Claus created its own special destiny. But it would take a while. The name was special, indeed, but no one really took advantage of the holiday possibilities until the local postmaster, one James Martin (the 14th postmaster, in, oddly enough, 1914) began to personally answer children's mail that came addressed simply to "Santa Claus." It didn't matter if these were the days before zip codes. Heck, the letters didn't even have to say "Indiana" anywhere. If the child simply wrote "Santa Claus" on the envelope or postcard, it eventually made its way to Santa Claus, Indiana. And the tradition has continued for nearly 100 years now. Local residents volunteer each Christmas season to personally answer each letter, free of charge, and the town holds fundraisers and accepts donations to cover the postage. It's a substantial undertaking, considering they annually answer over 10,000 letters to Santa!

Well, the story doesn't end with just answered letters. It seems a fine gentleman by the name of Louis Koch settled in the town around 1946. When his son returned from World War II, the two men decided to give children who came to the town of Santa Claus looking for the real Santa Claus (he must live in the town named after him, right?) some memories to go home with. What resulted was a small amusement park complete with rides, food vendors, and, of course, Santa Claus. Now consider this. We have all been told (it's a fact, right?) that Disneyland, which opened in California, was the first theme park in the United States. And I grant you, this is completely believable given Disneyland's size, scope, and fame. But in 1946, Louis Koch and his son opened a park themed on Santa and his North Pole, with holiday attractions and a Mother Goose Land for children, complete with a Candy Castle, an elf's factory, a village, and Santa Claus himself. By anybody's definition — that's a theme park! And it opened nine years before Disneyland.

Other folks saw the magic that the Santa connection could bring to the town. There were plans for larger parks and a competing petting zoo and picnic park, and a rival neighbor even went so far as to erect a huge 22-foot-tall concrete statue of Santa Claus dedicated "to the children of the world in an undying love," as the marker at its base reads, in 1935. It seems that by the 1930s and the 1940s, the whole town was starting to believe in Santa, one way or another.

Under the leadership and vision of the Koch family, Santa Claus Land prospered as a regional theme park in the 1950s and continued growing in the 1960s. It put the small, oddly named town on the map. Even today, when you visit the town's shopping center, visit the tall Santa statue, and close in on

Holiday World's impressive wooden roller coasters (you can see them for miles away as you drive through the countryside), it is possible to be overtaken by the fact that the town is still virtually in the middle of nowhere. Without both Santa Claus as a name and the theme park — the name Holiday World replaced Santa Claus Land when the park added two more themed lands for the Fourth of July and Halloween in the 1980s — the area probably would have devolved into a forgotten rural ghost town with a dilapidated drive-in screen and a couple of auto graveyards. Or far worse, had the Koch family had the unrestrained zeal and drive of some developers, the town and its surrounding fields could have become overgrown with chain hotels, attractions, souvenir shops, and giant discount centers. But it didn't. Santa Claus Land morphed into Holiday World to grow just enough to survive. The visitor to Spencer County, Indiana, today will be pleasantly surprised at how rural and homey this very large amusement park and its themed shopping center can be. It is truly a great way for a family to come to the hills and be a family again.

And must-stops along the way are the Santa Claus, Indiana, post office and the Kringle Plaza shopping center, with all of their wonderful exterior Santa décor. How many post offices in America have a Santa Claus outside holding their zip code sign year round? Also in the same plaza is the Santa Claus Museum, sponsored by Pat Koch, a third generation owner of all that is Santa Claus Land and Holiday World. There's even a charming young museum curator inside, Crystal Beuler. Crystal welcomed me when I first visited the museum and began my explanation about this book, its scope and why I needed to include the Santa folklore of the community in it. The museum is free and open to the public, and it houses some great old Santa collectibles in addition to priceless examples of the early history of Santa Claus Land. When you go there, be sure to ask Crystal about the program that sets into motion the answering of the more than 10,000 letters to Santa annually. It's an impressive showing of a small community joining together for the common good, with a not-so-common purpose — fulfilling the wishes of the world's children.

No matter how old you are, give Santa Claus, Indiana, a day of your time. The amusement park alone is worth the trip. The rolling rural countryside is unique and gorgeous any season of the year, and the Santa Claus museum is an extra highlight for devoted Santa lovers, no matter how young or old!

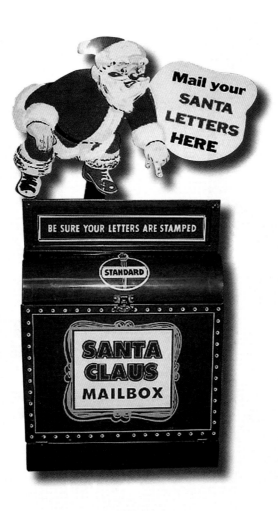

Santa Claus Land mug or stein.
$20.00 – 35.00.

Santa Claus Land teacup and saucer.
$65.00 – 100.00 for set.

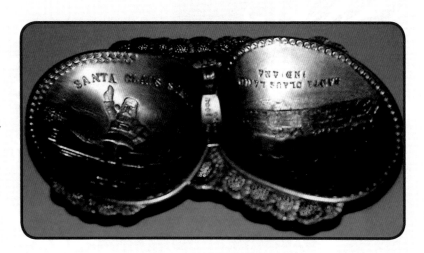

Santa Claus Land ashtray.
$25.00 – 45.00.

Santa Claus Land tiny pitcher from child's
tea set. $25.00 – 35.00.

Santa Claus Land souvenir china slipper
toothpick holder. $45.00 – 75.00.

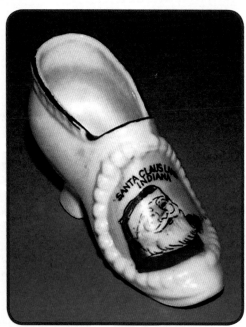

Giant doll and toy display in the Santa Museum.

Close-up view of the large Santa Claus doll in the museum at Santa Claus, Indiana.

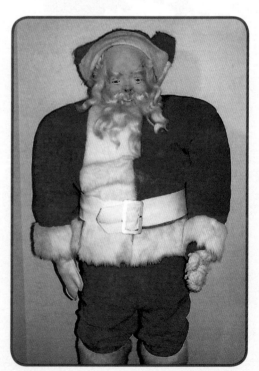

Unusual, giant 36" store display Santa in the museum. $800.00 – 1,200.00.

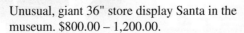

Santa Claus Land chalk or composition figural bank. $125.00 – 200.00.

Santa Claus Land official guidebook, vintage. $50.00 – 75.00.

Santa Claus Land early vintage promotional flyer. $25.00 – 35.00.

Promotional postcard. $10.00 – 15.00.

Vintage 1962 ad. $40.00 – 60.00.

Vintage original Holiday World art. $100.00 – 200.00.

Santa Claus Land tin lithographed child's tambourine. $75.00 – 100.00.

Santa Claus Land tin souvenir tray. $35.00 – 60.00.

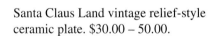

Santa Claus Land vintage relief-style ceramic plate. $30.00 – 50.00.

Framed early map. $100.00 – 150.00.

Candy Castle photograph, sketch, and Santa art, all in the same frame. $200.00 – 350.00.

Collection of three different Santa Claus mugs in the Santa Claus Museum.

Santa Claus Land, Indiana, roadside porcelain sign, rare. $700.00 – 1,000.00.

Santa Claus Museum sign.

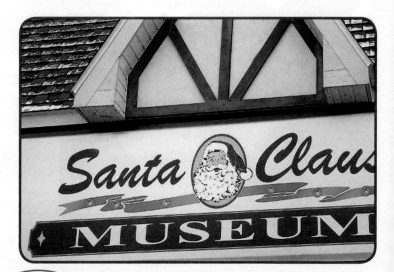

Santa Claus high atop display at Kringle Plaza.

Life-sized Santa figure at Kringle Plaza.

Santa Claus statue (life-sized) outside the Santa Claus Museum.

Detail of the Santa Claus statue at the Santa Claus Museum.

Santa Claus figure holding sign outside the famous U.S. Post Office at Santa Claus, Indiana (zip code 47579). The post office receives over 10,000 letters addressed to Santa each year, and Santa and his helpers *personally answer every one free of charge*. There is no fee for the letters, the return postmark, or the service!

Another view of the Post Office, famous for its Santa Claus postmark!

Crystal Buehler, the helpful and informative curator of the Santa Claus Museum at Santa Claus, Indiana.

The Santa Claus statue outside the Santa Claus Museum.

Santa Claus collectors all have one thing in common. They know that Santa is not just a December character. He lives in us year round. And the search for items in his likeness is not a December event, either. For successful Santa hunting, the trek must be endured 12 months out of the year. This small chapter will be devoted to that hunt, with advice along the way for seeking out both the old and the best of St. Nick, and also how to maintain your Christmas and Santa collections.

First and foremost, start close to home. Even the most advanced Santa collectors will usually admit that their first Santa pieces were those that were acquired from their own families, were those sentimental tokens of childhood Christmases past. Whether packed away in shoeboxes, antique trunks, attics, or basements, most of us found Santas from our younger years that were amazingly familiar, and we treasured those.

But the advanced collector knows that to piece together a world-class antique Santa Claus collection takes years of scouring antique shows and flea markets, and acquiring a nose for seeking out the very best examples.

One of the things I have discovered during 30 years of collecting is that good old Santas are often discovered in clusters. That is, if you find one good Santa somewhere, there are probably several others nearby. The reason for this is that rarely are antique Santa pieces pawned, sold off singly, or discarded. There is just too much emotional attachment to them. Usually, a group of old Santas may appear on the marketplace when a family's entire Christmas decoration assemblage is sold off, or when an heir who has inherited boxes of the treasures decides to let them go all at once. This usually means antique Santa dolls, toys, figures, candles, books, and decorations may hit the collector's marketplace together. And often, at antiques auctions, Santa items (even very early examples!) are sold as boxed lots.

The country auction is a great place to find old primitive examples dating from the turn of the last century. Certainly states like Pennsylvania and Ohio, and northeastern states in particular, are strong on the Santa potential list because so many of the great antique Santas were of German origin, and these states boast strong Germanic ancestry. German immigrants often brought great old Santas with them, from straw-filled dolls and rare bisques to composition and plaster Belsnickles (early figural Santas). Look to the north (as the saying goes) and take an easterly drift — there you will find Santas.

Established antique shows and elite auction houses are also excellent places to find old Santas, but prices are usually at a premium. If a dealer has already invested a sizable amount in a Santa piece and then added his own markup, bargains will be very hard to find.

To be honest, finding Santas when and where no one is looking for them will net you the best results. Only the devoted collectors seek out Santa in March and April when spring is on everyone's mind, and these are the months when the bargains can be found. In the spring months, even great antique Santa items can be purchased at bargain prices on eBay and other internet sales and auction sites. Why? Because the casual collector, designer, and antique speculator doesn't have the foggiest notion that the Christmas holiday season (which begins now in mid-November) is actually just six months away.

So, as a Santa collector for over three decades now, I offer the novice collector the following list of points to follow (and seasoned collectors can just join in and nod their heads):

1. Look for Santa collectibles in clusters. Find one Santa, and there are probably many more. He usually doesn't travel alone.

2. Seek out the Santas that have been passed down from family to family. Certainly start with your own. If there are elderly pack rats in your family tree who are still living and still have their life's possessions stored away, don't overlook the possibility that there might be a treasured box of Christmas heirlooms packed away somewhere. Do a little elfish detective work.

3. Look out for estate sales and country auctions where it appears that there was some affluence in the family. Santa decorations and figurines were luxuries, not Yuletide necessities. Often, the Christmas box lots and ornament storage boxes are some of the last things to sell at an auction because they are treated as last-minute extras. Don't overlook these box lots. Great old Santas from a hundred years ago might be found within!

4. Do not neglect the power of spreading the word. Many collectors are shy about talking about their collections or what they collect. Let people know what you are looking for, and you might be amazed at what turns up on your front door!

5. When buying Santa or Christmas collectibles on the internet, shop in the off-season of spring and let your PayPal account and checkbook rest as the holidays approach. Prices really do spike on holiday items in the three months leading up to Christmas.

6. If you are going to be devoted to Santa collecting for the long haul, then purchase your items in near-mint or mint condition. As your collection grows and your tastes change, you will never be disappointed in items that are in first-rate condition. Buy mint items, and you only have to buy once. You won't spend your life trying to find a better example and then be forced to unload what you shouldn't have purchased in the first place.

Now that you have made the commitment of time, energy, and dollars to collecting antique Santas, make sure that you take steps to protect your financial and emotional investments. First of all, film your entire collection, making sure to have audio. Record your thoughts about items in your collection, speak about their ultimate value, and do sweeping panoramic shots to show how and where your items are displayed, and then zoom in on your most valuable examples. Don't be shy! Narrate your video. This will be done for the security of your collection and your own peace of mind, so being bashful about the value or scope of your collection is not a wise thing to do on camera.

One of my best collecting friends keeps one copy of his collection video in his bank lockbox, one at home, and one hidden in his car at all times. At first, I thought this was an extremely cautious approach, but his retort was that the chances of his bank, his home, and his car all being destroyed at once were astronomical. I had to agree. Good plan, safe idea. Do it!

If your collection is worth more than $1,000 (not just one piece, your entire collection!) then it is time to itemize it, have it appraised, and insure it. Most insurance policies without an antiques or collectibles rider attached simply will insure the common replacement values of lost items. Example: If you lose a box of 12 antique Santa Claus ornaments in a fire or storm, most policies will give you the $10 or so it will take to buy twelve new, generic ornaments. They will not reimburse you the $1,200 value of the box because all of them were $100-a-piece hand-blown 1900s German examples.

Get the point? Most insurance riders cost just a few dollars a year per each $100 in value. This is a wise investment. Once again, my advice is to do it!

Few collectors consider the fragility of Santa items when faced with the possibility of a century-old antique being packed and unpacked over a hundred times. We tend to think in terms of just packing the item away "this year" quite nicely, and that will suffice. This is not the case. Each year, each packing and unpacking adds to the wear and tear on the item. If at all possible, display your Santa items year-round behind glass in a humidity-controlled environment. Basements (unless permanently dehumidified) are not suitable for the fragile materials of wool beards, felt costumes, and composition faces and hands that are found on many of the old Santa Claus collectibles treasured by collectors today.

If the passage of time and the seasonal packing and re-packing of items are negative stresses upon antique Santas, they are just the tip of the iceberg. Direct sunlight can particularly imperil antique Santa figures, especially those that are of painted composition, lithographed tin and paper, and wool or cloth construction. Never place your Santas in direct sunlight, because even indirect sunlight can be damaging. Displaying items as a collection behind glass is usually the safest bet, as the glass itself reflects away a portion of the harmful light rays. Sunlight can be particularly harmful to antique lithographed paper items and can damage them beyond measure in the short period of one or two Christmas seasons.

Another cause for concern is insects. Moths, beetles, and a slew of other muncher creatures seem to find the glues used in wood composition toys, dolls, and Santas a delicacy. They can devour a beautiful composition face or nose beyond recognition over a period of several days. A very fat moth once consumed the composition toes of a doll of mine in a showcase, and then ate away the paint on the doll's nose for dessert! I found him dead at the feet of the doll he had defaced, so at least he went out with a

very full stomach. It's not a perfect solution or deterrent, but since we are dealing with Santa Claus dolls and figures that often sport wool beards and wool felt clothes, a single moth ball placed near or behind the doll will usually do the trick, as long as it is out of the reach of children. And although even a single moth ball can stink, it is bearable and worth the trouble to prevent a rogue moth from entering a showcase by chance and doing irreparable harm.

Generally, what's best for humans is also best for your Santa collectibles. Try to store your keepsakes, decorations, and treasures in parts of the house that are both temperature and humidity controlled. Basements and attics, where these items are most commonly stored, are not the best for them. Try to get a little creative as to where else you might store your Santa treasures. With that in mind, they will certainly last for another century or two, and additional family generations.

Collector Contacts

Readers who desire to contact any of the contributors to this book may do so care of my P.O. box address, or may write me directly. Please include a self-addressed stamped envelope if you would like a mailed reply. My address is David Longest, P.O. Box 2183, Clarksville, Indiana 47131. Send the name of the collector you would like to contact at the top of the address, and I will forward it to the particular collector. The principal collector who contributed to this book, Diane Savage, maintains her own email and can be reached directly at the email address listed with her name.

DIANE SAVAGE — Advanced collector of Santa Claus collectibles and the principal contributor (she contributed *many* items) to this book. Collectors with questions, items for sale, or other comments may write her directly at her email address, which is dinet94611@comcast.net.

CHARLES "BUTCH" and LINDA MILLER — Advanced collectors of primitive folk-art Santas and Victorian-era very early Santa examples. They also collect antique children's items, children's books predating the turn of the century, and antique Christmas ornaments. Write to them care of the author's address above.

KEN and KATHY RAYMOND — Also advanced collectors of very early Christmas items, both Ken and Kathy work in the printing and graphics design world, so unique early items are what catch their eye. They are also, on occasion, dealers in very fine antiques. If you have something unusual, write to them care of the author's address above.

JIM and BONNIE KASARI — Collectors of Christmas Coca-Cola items with Santa graphics, and some general Christmas nutcrackers and designer items. Their taste leans toward newer Santa and Coca-Cola items. Write to them care of the author.

JEANNE WEAVER — Collector extraordinaire of very old antique Santas. Jean has also been an antiques dealer all of her life, so if you have something very old, and very Santa, you may write to her care of the author.

ELMER and VIOLA REYNOLDS — Lifelong friends of the author, Elmer and Viola specialize in old-time comic character toys, but they also collect Coca-Cola ads with Santa and Victorian Santa examples. They welcome correspondence, care of the author.

CHARLOTTE DOUGLAS and TOM LUCE — General antiques, Disneyana, and Santa collectors can correspond care of the author.

Contact for the SANTA CLAUS MUSEUM pictured in chapter 5:
Crystal Buehler, Director
Santa Claus Museum
41 North Kringle Place P.O. Box 1
Santa Claus, IN 47579

Phone: 812-937-2687
Email: scmcurator@psci.net
Website: www.santaclausmuseum.org

Contact to write SANTA directly, via Santa Claus, Indiana:
Santa Claus
P.O. Box 1
Santa Claus, IN 47579

ABOUT THE AUTHOR

David Longest is the author of eight previous books on collecting antiques published by Collector Books: *Character Toys and Collectibles* (1984); *Character Toys and Collectibles, Series Two* (1986); *Toys — Antique and Collectible* (1988); *The Collector's Encyclopedia of Disneyana* (with Michael Stern, 1991); *Antique Toys, 1870 to 1960* (1993); *Cartoon Toys and Collectibles* (1997); *Collecting Disneyana* (2007); and *The Collector's Toy Yearbook* (2007). David is proud to have been a Collector Books author for 26 years!

Longest has written nationally for *Collector's Showcase Magazine*, *Antique Trader Magazine*, the *Tri-State Trader*, and *Antique Toy World Magazine*, and served as a monthly feature writer and contributing editor for *Toy Shop Magazine* in the 1990s.

David's full-time job is serving as a teacher and director of theatre at New Albany High School in Indiana, where he is an award-winning teacher with an award-winning theatre program. His program was awarded the National Outstanding High School Theatre Award by the Educational Theatre Association in 2004, and he was selected as the New Albany Floyd County Teacher of the Year and was an Indiana Teacher of the Year Semi-Finalist, also in 2004. David is, additionally, the recipient of two Lily Endowment Teacher Creativity Awards and the WHAS-TV Excel Award for Outstanding Teaching. He is also one of the only high school teachers in the nation to ever win the prestigious National American History Medal awarded by the Daughters of the American Revolution in Washington, D.C. He won the award for co-authoring an original musical on Lewis and Clark, and for his adaptation of *Little Women,* which was published by Dramatic Publishing of Chicago, Illinois. Last summer, David was honored with a Presidential Scholar Teacher Recognition Award by the U.S. Department of Education in Washington, D.C. He has been a guest lecturer on Broadway in New York for Broadway Classroom, and he and his students were featured in three full pages of the *New York Times* in May of 2005. Additionally, David Longest and his students are soon to be featured in a 2008 documentary to be released by Lions Gate Pictures of Hollywood and Showtime television and directed by film director Barry Blaustein. The documentary focuses on exemplary high school musical theatre programs.

David is a lifelong resident of Indiana and has enjoyed collecting Santa and Christmas collectibles with his wife, Ann, and daughter, Claire, for the past 30 years.

Since 1946, millions upon millions of families have treasured the memories they've created first at Santa Claus Land and then at Holiday World & Splashin' Safari. This Santa Claus Land ad is from the early 1980s. The park's name was changed to Holiday World in 1984, but so much is still the same. Family-owned and -operated since opening, Holiday World & Splashin' Safari in Santa Claus, Indiana, put families first, with free soft drinks, free parking, free sunscreen and award-winning hospitality. For more information, call 1-877-Go-Family or visit www.HolidayWorld.com.

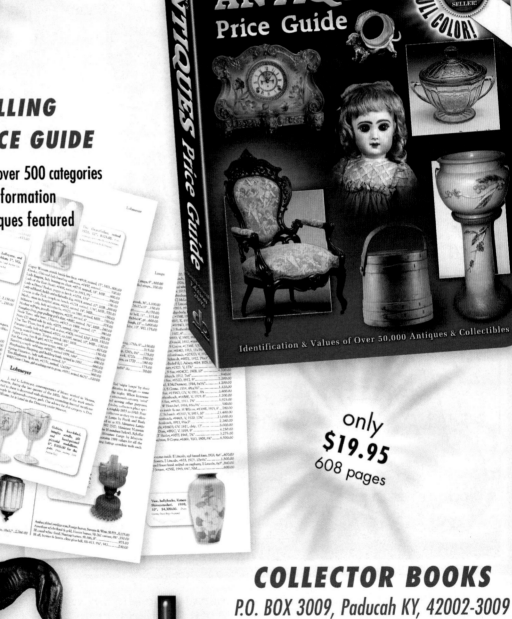